Sarah Shears

A Village Girl

MEMOIRS OF
A KENTISH CHILDHOOD

Introduction by
R. F. DELDERFIELD

Simon and Schuster · New York

*This book is dedicated
in loving appreciation
of a Good Mother*

Contents

The Short and Simple Annals

Occasionally, possibly once every decade, the English literary scene is enriched by a piece of writing that glows with truth like a cottage lamp set down among a cluster of neon lights. Do not be persuaded that this is other than a rare occurrence. Publishers, public, and reviewers alike are all too familiar with the spate of pretentious nonsense spewing, week by week, from a hundred would-be James Joyces, and twice as many would-be D. H. Lawrences. Especially the reading public, who can be relied upon, more than their mentors, to recognize truth when it leaps from the printed page.

There is a pattern to this occasional visitation. In almost every case it is woven around childhood memories that have lain dormant in the mind of a modest and sometimes self-educated person waiting—often for half a century—to emerge and be spun into fiction, autobiography, or a mixture of both. The backdrop is invariably humble, perhaps a manufacturing town, an unfashionable suburb, a remote mountain valley, the kind of place where truth is apt to take root and grow, where one is not encouraged to put on airs, literary or otherwise, where the streets and lanes and bypaths are sign-posted by old-fashioned virtues—neighborliness, courage, uncomplaining endurance, resilience, warmth, and honesty or, if you prefer it, decency-plus-guts.

Miss Sarah Shears' unvarnished record of about nine years from her early life in a Kentish village is such a book, one of the most touching I have ever read. I recommend it to anyone who is looking for the secret of what life is all about, what makes real people tick, what really constitutes character.

It is a book entirely without artifice. And yet, in its quiet way, it is a work of art, because the warp and weft of its material is instantly recognizable as hard fact by anyone whose memories go back to the years of the First World War, to an era when life for the poor and underprivileged was not much better endowed than it was in the first flush of the Industrial Revolution.

Sarah was the second child and elder daughter of a will-of-a-wisp sergeant major (who spent no more than six months with the family in the span of years recounted) and a woman whose hardihood and essential nobility of character have earned her, I hope, a privileged seat among the elect. The mother dominates the book, a woman of such strength of character and such steadfastness of purpose that she could serve as a living example of the beatitudes put into practice. Left with four young children to bring up, and no source of income beyond her stores of matchless courage and rigid self-discipline, she moves through the pages of Miss Shears' book like Boadicea riding out in her chariot to do battle with the Romans. She is there all the time, sometimes in the foreground, sometimes in the background, scrimping, saving, devising, correcting, training, hoping, believing, through a sixteen-hour day that would close any factory in the Western world were it imposed upon employees for a week, much less nine long (and largely happy) years. And yet, for all her singularity, she is typical of her class and generation, and if you doubt that, look beyond the mother to some of Miss Shears' other scenes—the Kentish hop fields, milling with gypsies and East End cockneys, the village sweetshop where the proprietress *encouraged* customers with a halfpenny to spend to take their time making up their minds, to the homes of neighbors and friends, to Sunday School picnics, to the village school, the local vicarage, indeed, anywhere Miss Shears takes you on her odyssey from the age of five to the day she came out of a London hospital after three major operations at fourteen-plus.

Every scene and every character is etched with truth and a child's candid and often diabolically accurate observation. We meet the grandmother and her five unmarried daughters, the chicken-farming lodger "Uncle" John, a lovable piece of flotsam salvaged from the hell of the Western Front, the snobs up at the country houses and vicarage who absorbed these village children like so many Oliver Twists, and a whole complex of society in one tiny corner of a land where welfare, as we know it in 1970, did not exist and would almost certainly have been dismissed in blueprint as "mollycoddling," or an affront to the dignity of the working class. It is a world as far removed from a majority today as the world of Agincourt and the Luddites, but, for all its cruelties and gross injustices, it had a quality. It is Miss Shears' triumph that she makes you aware of this quality and—dare one say it?—the smallest bit nostalgic for its absence fifty years later. Yet it must have been in the mind of the poet Gray when he sat in Stoke Poges churchyard and wrote:

> *Let not ambition mock their useful toil,*
> *Their homely joys and destiny obscure;*
> *Nor grandeur hear with a disdainful smile*
> *The short and simple annals of the poor.*

R. F. DELDERFIELD

11

1
The Village School

We stopped on the way to buy my first hoop. They were sold in three sizes and I wanted the largest but had to "make do" with the smallest—price three-pence—because we always had to "make do" and it didn't surprise me.

Mother was blunt and strictly practical. "We will take the small one, thank you," she said.

"But it hasn't got a stick!" I wailed.

"We will find a stick in the hedge on the way to school," Mother said firmly.

"But I don't want a hedge stick, I want a proper stick, with a nail, like William's."

"Only boys have sticks with nails, because their hoops are made of iron, and girls' hoops are made of wood."

"It's not fair!" I grumbled.

"Well, do you want the hoop, Sarah? Make up your mind. Yes or no. Quickly!"

"I want it."

Miss Baker patted my head and handed over the hoop.

"Such lovely children! How I envy you," she said, and Mother frowned and shook her head reprovingly, for I had already started to preen myself in the mirror.

"I'm starting school today," I told Miss Baker importantly. "I'm five. Why do you wear your gloves indoors?"

"Not gloves dear, mittens," she corrected primly. "My chilblains, dear. I get them every winter."

"So I do, on my toes."

"*So do I,*" Mother prompted automatically.

(Did Mother have chilblains, then, but I had never seen them?)

But she dragged me away quickly, before I could ask any more embarrassing questions, for it was rumored that Miss Baker also wore a wig!

William, aged seven, was breathing on the windowpane and drawing faces with a wet glove.

His sou'wester had slipped over one ear and he had completely forgotten he was in charge of the pram and the little ones, Mary and Henry. The pram was lodged precariously against a doorstep.

But Mother never panicked.

"Oh, *William!*" she exclaimed in sheer exasperation. He turned his handsome dark head and shrugged his small shoulders and went on breathing his hot breath on the windowpane, because he had only a mild curiosity and no affection, as yet, for his younger sisters and baby brother.

14

We had no time now to hunt for a stick, so I bowled my new hoop with my hand.

"Come along, William!" called Mother urgently as the school bell started to ring, while Mary (who never cried, and was always good) peered out from under her bonnet to watch the hoop spinning along the wet pavement.

The cloakroom, wet with puddles and uncomfortably damp and chilly, was crammed with children, all fighting for a peg on which to hang their coats and hats.

My brother William, already a scholar for two years, dived under the legs of a senior boy, grabbed a peg, and turned, scowling, to confront him.

"It's mine!" he cried triumphantly.

Mother smiled behind her gloved hand. I think she would have been a little ashamed if her eldest son had not found a peg, or called upon her to help. But I clung to her hand, trembling with fear and dislike of this strange new battleground, so far removed from our quiet kitchen, where fighting and quarrelling were never permitted, and rude, bad-tempered, or naughty children were sent to bed.

I began to cry, and William, seeing my tears, stopped scowling at the other boy and became surprisingly protective.

"You can share my peg, Sarah—just for today," he told me graciously and explained to the gaping children, "She's only five. She's just started."

I was so impressed by his performance I stopped crying, and Mother unbuttoned my coat, untied my bonnet, and smoothed my long thick hair with a firm hand.

"She'll be all right, but keep an eye on her, William —just for today," she added, for William was scowling again.

They left me at the door of the Infants' School, still clinging to my new hoop and the hand of my new teacher—Miss Bennett.

Shy and bewildered, I clung to the hoop and refused to part with it all that day. William had been swallowed up in the Big Children's School, and I did not see him again till twelve o'clock, when he rushed me into a small classroom and sat me down forcefully on a form near the fire, with a mug of cocoa and a thick cheese sandwich.

"I want to go home!" I wailed.

In good weather we went home to dinner, but in bad weather we stayed at school, he explained irritably, and added under his breath "Shut up!"

We sat in pairs on tiny chairs, sharing a tiny table and a tray of sand in the Infants' after dinner.

The sand was soft, like the sand we gave to Chips, our canary, and we had to pretend it was a desert— though nobody knew what a desert was, anyway. We also had to pretend that an ivy leaf was a palm tree, and a small potato with matchstick legs was a camel.

Into the lid of a cocoa tin we were allowed to pour a few drops of water for a pool. This pool and palm, we were told importantly by the imaginative Miss Bennett, was an *oasis*—a curious word that I repeated to myself over and over again, for I liked it better than the *cat* and *mat* on the teacher's blackboard.

Words fascinated me, from that very first day at school, and *oasis* was the only thing I remembered to tell Mother when she collected me at four o'clock.

In the middle of the Infants' classroom stood a massive stove that was stoked up with coke by the caretaker, morning and evening. It was so warm and stuffy in the schoolroom, we all became very sleepy, so we were allowed to fold our arms on the little tables, lay our heads down, and go to sleep. Miss Bennett seemed not to mind in the least that only half her pupils were attending to the lesson while the rest were fast asleep!

She sat me next to a girl called Evelyn, who was six years old and a "monitor" for that week.

Evelyn handed around slates and chalks, collected up the sand trays, and took us to the lavatory when we asked to be "excused"—I was so impressed by her authority, I asked to be excused four times that afternoon!

Only six girls, I noticed, including Evelyn and myself, wore white pinafores; the rest had colored pinafores, and some were dirty and torn. I also wore a pair of new black button boots, and long black stockings fastened to a "liberty bodice," with thick fleecy-lined bloomers under my skirt. My long shining hair (soon to be tied tightly into two plaits because of the danger of catching head lice) was adorned with a large flat bow of ribbon on top of my head, and I wore a little silver locket that contained a miniature of my grandmother.

Our first teacher was small and neat, with a shy smile and a soft voice. She sprinkled eau de cologne on her handkerchief. I loved her from the moment she took my hand, kissed my sulky mouth, and said gently, "But of course you can keep your hoop, dear."

She taught me how to skip, continuously, without pausing at every turn of the rope. This to me was a real achievement, for I had been trying to skip properly for months and months.

In the school playground, we all stood to attention

on Empire Day to sing as best we could—for the words were long and difficult to pronounce—"Land of Hope and Glory," while the Union Jack fluttered in the breeze and mothers gazed wet-eyed at their offspring over the wall and wondered about the war.

It was a village of women and children then, for this vague, unpleasant thing called "war" had taken all our fathers and uncles and elder brothers, and we had only their letters, very rare and very precious, read aloud and cried over, to remind us of their existence. As time went on—two, three, four years—and they did not return, it seemed that they no longer belonged to us, and we children lost interest in their letters and would not have cared if they never came back at all.

I do remember, though, I was pleased and proud when Mother allowed me to take a small sandalwood camel to school one day. (She had a collection of animals, vases, daggers, and odd-looking curios which my father had sent from Mestopotamia.) The little sandalwood camel was much admired, and each child in turn borrowed it for the sand tray, where it sheltered under the "palm tree" and drank from the pool in the cool *oasis!*

A status symbol in the Infants' School was provided by a simple pocket handkerchief. If you had one, you were considered a little superior to those who had only an odd scrap of rag, bundled into their sleeves, while those who wiped their dirty noses on their sleeves were utterly despised. A large clean handkerchief was pinned to my pinafore every day, because I had no pockets as yet in my clothes. To my mother's dismay, I spat on one corner to clean my slate, and she afterwards provided me with a small sponge.

We had prayers every morning and a hymn, with frequent lessons in scripture, in which we learned to repeat parrotwise the Lord's Prayer, the Twenty-third Psalm, and the story of Samuel.

It was a "church school," our teacher explained carefully, and the Vicar was our "governor," so we all must remember to say our prayers at night, to be good, obedient children, and then we should all go to Heaven.

"I don't *want* to go to Heaven—I want to go *home!*" I wailed.

The long hard winter that first year at school seemed to drag on endlessly, and my body and mind became so numb with the cold I could not remember anything else but snow and ice and frosted windowpanes.

Spring and summer had passed into a kind of vacuum, so far removed from our frozen fingers and frozen pipes that they had no meaning for me at all. The splendid pictures on the calendar, which Mother turned over from time to time for our inspection, I examined politely, but felt no interest or response. These little lambs, so joyfully gamboling in green meadows, were heavenly lambs—and surely I had never seen them in the fields of Kent. These lovely gardens, with their gay herbaceous borders and dancing daffodils—were they real? And apple blossom, pink and white, in glorious profusion, spread carelessly over a clear blue sky and fruit, ripe and luscious, hanging from the branches of all the trees in the months of August and September— surely I had never tasted such fruit, only an occasional orange when I had a sore throat, or a tangerine at Christmastime.

"But you have, you have, silly child!" Mother declared with some irritation, for she was so strong, so sturdy, so practical and no-nonsensical, so unconscious of fancies and fairies, wizards and witches.

She herself had a remarkable and prodigious memory and could tell you the names and birthdays of all the members of the Royal Family for three generations; the exact state of the weather on Easter Day last year; the day I cut my first tooth; and the changes of the moon—without even a peep at *Old Moore's Almanack!*

"But you must remember, Sarah. You can't have forgotten those lovely picnics in the hayfield last summer, and the woods where you played hide-and-seek with Mary in the tall bracken."

I shook my head sadly, for my mind was a complete blank.

"What's the matter with you, child?" she demanded anxiously. "Are you sick? Have you got another stomachache?"

"I'm cold," I told her truthfully.

"You had better have a dose of Syrup-of-Figs," she decided, for she had profound faith in the merits of this sweet and sickly medicine for children.

I pulled a face and backed away.

"I don't want it. I'm not sick and I haven't got a stomachache."

"Open your mouth!" She poured it quickly down my throat, and I shuddered with distaste.

"Why do you always make such a fuss about everything, Sarah? No medicine could be nicer to take than Syrup-of-Figs. Now, *when we were children* (I've heard all this before, I thought disrespectfully), we had to take horrid licorice powder once a week, and even castor oil."

I went on shuddering and shivering, for castor oil

was something so appallingly slimy and oily, any number of lies were permitted to postpone a dose.

"I've been," I would say doggedly. "Twice," I added for good measure.

"Sarah, are you telling me the truth?" Mother would insist.

But at that crucial moment, the baby, Henry, snug in his pram in the corner of the kitchen, would open his mouth and yell for attention.

He always did this and would go on yelling till someone picked him up. He was a fat, bouncing baby—quite unlike the rest of us—always hungry yet never satisfied, and he demanded more than his share of attention.

Mother sighed as she scooped him out of the pram and dropped a kiss on his damp fair head, but his wide blue eyes, swimming with tears a moment ago, were smiling now.

I knew what I had to do without being reminded, so I pulled out the old hassock from under the kitchen table and sat down, carefully spreading my skirt to make a lap.

Henry filled the lap so entirely I was almost completely submerged and could no longer see the fire or feel its warmth. But the bundle of baby warmed me, for he was wrapped like a papoose in long flannel petticoats, with woolly jackets and a shawl.

We all had worn these clothes and been wrapped in this shawl in turn and slept in the same pram. Indeed, nothing was new, for me or for Mary or for Henry, but only for William—because he was the first-born, and something very special and precious.

This I fully realized and understood right from the

21

start, and I had carefully explained it to Mary one day, but she only smiled and blew me a kiss and went on playing with her doll.

So I cuddled Henry until I began to wilt.

"I'm squashed! Take him back," I pleaded urgently.

Mother dried her wet hands, took the baby in her arms, and sat down in the sagging armchair beside the fire.

Quietly she unbuttoned her blouse, her camisole, and her combinations to suckle him at her breast.

Then she looked at me, sitting small and still and subdued on the hassock, and her stern face relaxed into a smile of infinite sweetness and joy; her dark eyes, soft as velvet, included me in that satisfying moment, and I loved her then and forgot the medicine and all my misery during that long hard winter.

Wrapped together, the three of us, in this warm intimacy, undisturbed by either of the others, I was happy again.

Such moments were rare and very precious.

"My mother is a Lady," I had told my first teacher during my first week at school.

"You mean she is lady*like*, dear."

"No, she's a *Lady!*" I protested stubbornly.

Miss Bennett smiled kindly and shook her head. "Only the Gentry are Ladies and Gentlemen, dear— the rest of us are just ordinary men and women."

What did she mean? I didn't understand.

Mother always wore her hat and gloves, even when she went to the grocer's, and she never said a swear word, and she had the nicest manners of anyone I knew

—and we wiped our noses on clean pocket handkerchiefs! If William said our mother was a Lady she was a Lady, for William was seven, and he knew simply Everything and I believed every word he said, without question.

On the third Thursday of every month, the District Nurse visited the Village School to examine the girls' heads—for lice. We lined up in the Infants' waiting our turn, wondering a little fearfully what to expect from this large masculine woman in her crackling white apron, smelling strongly of carbolic.

"What's *lice?*" I inquired of Evelyn, who had been through it all before.

She covered her mouth with her hand and whispered surreptitiously, "Shush!—they've got them!"

I turned around, eager to know more, and met the blank stares of the two little Smith sisters, who belonged to a large family of gypsies camped in a field at Bailey's Farm, waiting for the spring—they had four brothers in the Big School. They were never clean, these children, and their clothes and bodies had a peculiar earthy smell, rather like mushrooms. But they had the biggest, blackest eyes I had ever seen, and long straight hair, black like the wings of the blackbird William had brought home one day to make a splint for its broken wing.

"But where is the *lice?*" I persisted.

"In their hair, stupid!"

"I can't see it."

"It's not it, it's them—they've got *swarms*, and they will be sent home, see?"

I began to shiver and shake.

"You mean, crawling like caterpillars?"

"No, like fleas."

"*Fleas!*" I began to itch and scratch, remembering the night I itched so terribly I threw off all the bed-clothes and shouted for Mother. We had chased a tiny dark object by candlelight, but it got away and came back again and again to torment me.

"But shouldn't we see them hopping about?" I whispered hoarsely.

"Head fleas don't hop, silly, they crawl, and they make a lot of nits, and then you get more fleas," she added, with profound knowledge.

"What are *nits?*" I was really worried now.

"You're one, if you don't know!" she jeered.

"Quiet, girls, if you please," called Miss Bennett from the blackboard, where she was surrounded by the boys, all looking very smug and superior because their hair was too short to attract any lice.

"Evelyn," I pleaded, for I was desperately anxious to keep her friendship, with this impending disaster. "S'posing we get fleas in our heads—just s'posing?"

"I told you, silly, it's only dirty children. We are much too clean!"

"Well, and who have we here?" boomed a hearty voice, jabbing me playfully with a pair of sharp knitting needles. "We are not likely to find anything interesting in this beautiful head of hair, now are we?"

A cold shiver ran down my spine as she poked my head with the needles. My hair ribbon slid to the floor, but I was too stunned to pick it up.

Some weeks later, I ran home to Mother as fast as my short legs could carry me, burst into the kitchen, and cried out desperately, "I *itch!* In my *head.*"

Mother carefully put her big heavy iron back on the stove, and blew hard on my frozen fingers.

"Silly child, and all this fuss for nothing, I'm sure. Haven't I told you repeatedly, Sarah, that only dirty children get fleas in their hair?"

"But *look*, you must *look*," I pleaded, snatching off my bonnet.

She sighed, for there was so much work still to be done before nightfall, and when Henry woke from his afternoon nap, she would have to carry him around on her hip and do everything with one hand, or he screamed till he was blue in the face.

"Go upstairs and look in the brush and comb bag hanging on the washstand in my room. In it you will find the small-tooth comb I use for Mary's hair because it is so fine. Bring it down."

I ran so quickly to obey her instructions I was back with the comb before she had time to pick up the iron.

"Now, a clean towel to spread on my lap." I snatched one from the clothes line and knelt between her knees, and she spread my hair all over her lap and combed carefully and silently till I heard a sudden gasp of dismay burst from her lips, and I parted my hair and peered out to gaze in fascinated horror at a small dark insect on the white towel.

"A *flea!* A *flea!*" I shrieked.

Mother quickly recovered from the shock, picked up the offending creature disdainfully, and dropped it into the fire.

"Now listen to me, Sarah—it's gone, it's finished, so stop crying."

She spoke quietly and authoritatively, but I was not convinced.

"*Nits*," I wailed miserably. "They make little nits, and then you get swarms of fleas—Evelyn told me so."

"I should like to shake this Evelyn, she is not a nice child," Mother declared, searching every inch of hair.

"Will they know about me at school? Shall I be sent home, like Sybil and Annie Smith and Martha Kent?"

"Of course not, child. Nobody will know unless you tell them—but I shall see Miss Bennett in the morning, confidentially. This is disgraceful! Those gypsy children should not be allowed to mix with decent respectable children."

"*Do* something, you must *do* something so they never come back," I persisted.

She mopped my tears and tied on my bonnet.

"Where are we going?" I wanted to know.

She looked down at me with gentle forbearance and smiled tolerantly. "To buy some ointment that will frighten the fleas away."

"Magic ointment?"

"Magic ointment," she repeated, to pacify her fanciful young daughter.

Then she gathered up Mary, warmly wrapped in a blanket, and popped her under the hood of the pram with Henry, still mercifully sleeping.

On the kitchen table she left a printed note for William, who was invariably late home from school:

TAKE OFF WET BOOTS. GET TEA READY. DO NOT TOUCH FIRE. BACK SOON.

MOTHER.

The snowplow had piled up the snow into solid walls on either side of the road, and we walked briskly back to the village, pushing the heavy pram over the slippery icy surface, while fresh tears froze on my

cheeks as the combined misery of the flea and the frost
became too intolerable to bear.

I never mentioned the flea to anyone—I was too
ashamed, and, surprisingly, the secret never leaked out,
and I never saw another.

"What's that ugly thing you are making?" William
demanded one evening.

"A Balaclava helmet—for you, William," Mother
replied without lifting her head.

William snorted, "I shan't wear it!"

"You will wear it, William," said Mother firmly,
looking him straight in the eyes.

William shuffled uncomfortably but glared back,
and I noticed for the first time that his eyes were bold
and black, like Mother's, when he was angry or annoyed, but the color of chocolate when he was pleased
and happy.

"Your father wears a Balaclava helmet in the
winter, exactly like this one. I knitted it for him last
winter."

Mother dropped her eyes to her knitting again and
said no more. William considered the matter gravely,
with his hands thrust deep in his pockets. His sturdy
legs, set wide apart on the hearthrug, left no room at
the fireside for Sarah or for Mary. We sat hunched
together on the hassock, watching him closely with
adoring eyes.

"It's not bad," he admitted grudgingly and added,
"But I'm not wearing it on Sunday."

"Of course not, William," Mother agreed quietly.

"I want a Balaclava," I reminded her quickly, before she used up all the wool.

"You shall have the next one, Sarah, because you are getting too big for a bonnet. Navy blue for girls, and khaki for boys," she explained slyly to William.

He grinned back at her, well pleased.

But I didn't care much for the Balaclava helmet when it was ready to wear, for the wool was harsh and tickled my chin, and I wished I was back in my cozy little bonnet. William was right, of course, and it was ugly, and I looked hideous in mine when it got stuck over one eye or nearly gagged me! William lost his during a snowball fight and never had another.

"You are much too fastidious," Mother told me one day when I had refused to wear a pinafore only slightly soiled.

"*Fastidious?*—that's a lovely word!" I told her, delighted to add it to my short vocabulary. "Can you tell me some more lovely long words?"

"You're a strange child, Sarah," she sighed as she helped me to button up the pinafore from behind. "I don't know where you get these fanciful notions, certainly not from me, or your father either.

"Now if it was music, I could understand it better," she went on thoughtfully. "Your grandmother, on my side of the family, is very musical. She played the piano beautifully when she was only as old as William—so clever and talented, and an only child, too, with a most expensive education—and then to run away from home to marry a poor farmer." Mother gazed sadly over the top of my head, across the distant valley, and her eyes were wistful.

"Mother, why don't you want me to say big words? Is it wicked?"

She turned from the window to smile at me, and her rare smile warmed my heart, as her hot breath had warmed my frozen fingers.

"Of course it's not wicked, child, but people will laugh at you if you don't know the meaning of big words, and little girls should use little words."

She looked at my downcast face and added kindly, "But you can always ask me or your teacher, can't you?"

I gave her a grateful hug and ran off to play with my hoop.

Five minutes later I was back to ask, "Mother, what *is fastidious?*"

"*Fussy!* Now run away and play like a good girl."

"Fastidious—fastidious—fastidious," I sang as I whacked my hoop down the lane.

The long, long winter was over at last. The snow had melted, the icicles thawed, and the frosted window-panes were no longer painted by Jack Frost with silver leaves and stars. The grass was surprisingly green under the snow, and nothing had died, not even the snowdrops. I couldn't understand how they had managed to live all winter under a thick blanket of snow, when they were almost too fragile to touch. William, perhaps, could solve this new mystery.

But he was engaged on his own particular problem, and wouldn't care to be disturbed—the problem of arranging his large and varied assortment of prewar cigarette cards to the best advantage in the new album Mother had given him for his eighth birthday.

He frowned at me when I interrupted his fierce concentration on the matter in hand, as I so often did these days. I repeated the question twice, however, with my usual persistence and stood waiting patiently for an answer until he was ready to give me his attention. I was so accustomed to waiting for William to notice me, I was not at all upset by his lack of interest.

He continued to frown at the cards that he had collected from the butcher and the grocer and the grave-digger—for we lived near the church, and the grave-digger was a prodigious smoker of Black Cat.

I knew William already had a complete set of wild birds, for he had allowed me to look, but not to touch, as a special treat, and he told me their names and the color of their eggs.

"What did you say?" he asked carelessly, looking up at last.

I repeated the question for the third time.

"Snowdrops?" he asked scornfully. "Who cares about snowdrops?"

"I do."

"You care about the stupidest things, Sarah!"

I wondered what he meant.

"But you're not such a cry baby as you used to be when you were little," he added graciously.

That was praise indeed from William, and I glowed with pride and there and then decided never to cry again.

"You honestly don't know?—cross your heart and hope to die."

I crossed my heart and hoped to die if I was not speaking the truth.

"Snowdrops don't stay there all the winter, silly. They stay inside."

"Inside where?" I persisted.

"Inside the bulb!" he shouted. "Now go away and stop asking me silly questions. *Go away.*"

We hadn't room for a garden, and we had only a back yard, so what was a bulb?

How did the snowdrop live inside it all winter?

And how did it get out in the spring?

My teacher answered all three questions by actually showing the class a bunch of snowdrops she had picked in her garden and a cluster of small shriveled objects which she had carefully dug up to explain their mysterious growth. It was my first nature lesson and I was fascinated by this wonderful new discovery.

"Please, teacher, how do they get out?" I asked anxiously (when she had stopped talking, for it was rude to interrupt). She was never surprised by anything and always delighted to have our full attention.

"That's a very good question, Sarah. Can anyone in the class tell Sarah how the snowdrop gets out of the bulb?"

"No, teacher," they chorused.

"Then I will tell you. *God lets the snowdrop out.*"

God? I was still puzzled, and still unsatisfied, for if God lived in Heaven, and Heaven was up in the sky, how could He see the tiny snowdrop waiting to get out of the bulb?

But, since everyone, including teacher, seemed perfectly happy with that simple explanation, we went on with the next question.

Nature lesson, however, had taken the place of sand trays, and every Tuesday afternoon for the rest of the year we explored the surrounding fields and examined hedges, trees, and flowers and came back to the classroom with "specimens" to draw on our slates.

31

The Infants' School was overflowing with new pupils, and Miss Bennett was nearly at her wit's end, for she hadn't enough chairs and tables to seat them all comfortably.

"We must weed out a few of the brighter children for Standard One," the Headmaster decided.

"Well, if you insist, sir, but they are not really ready for Standard One, and not yet seven years of age."

"Nevertheless, it must be done."

Miss Bennett flushed and wrung her hands, for the truth of the matter was, of course, that she couldn't bear to part with any of her children.

William had told me horrifying stories of Standard One and the teacher, known as the "Dragon," so I tried to hide behind Evelyn.

"I will call out the names of the children, and will they please step forward."

The soft voice we loved so well was strangely husky.

"Evelyn Parker, William Foster, Thomas Bond, Beryl Chantry, Emily Mason, and Sarah Shears."

2
Two Eggs Between Four of Us

"Father is a Regimental Sergeant Major," William informed me importantly one day in 1916. "If the Dragon asks you about Father, and she will, you know, because she's always asking silly questions about our parents, you have to answer up smartly, or she gets mad."

"Then tell me again, slowly, please, William." For I was already scared to death of the Dragon.

Her malicious tongue was most cruel to the youngest and most defenseless of her pupils, for they had been coddled and cosseted in the Infants' School for so long that they were not prepared, in spite of warnings from the older children.

"My father is a Regimental Sergeant Major. My father is a Regimental Sergeant Major," I repeated dutifully after William.

It certainly sounded very grand, but I was more

worried about having to tell the Dragon. I no longer went to school with eager and joyful anticipation, wondering what our kind and gentle teacher had in store for us and whether it would be my proud privilege to be monitor—handing out the colored chalks and slates, wiping the blackboard with a clean duster, and taking the little ones to the lavatory. Miss Bennett had made us all feel so very special and so very important, thinking our slow progress quite remarkable, and telling us so. Her warm praise was never sparing, and her soft voice never raised in anger. Had we left an Angel to battle with a Devil? Had we no weapons at all?

"Move back one form, all the children in the class —quickly!" we heard her say. "I want the new batch of Infants in the front row, under my observation."

Her voice sounded harsh and loud as we came slowly and shyly through the door, with Miss Bennett heading the sad little procession, leading me by the hand.

The swift glance that passed between the two teachers was hostile, for they disliked each other intensely, and we all knew about it from our elder brothers and sisters. "The Dragon would scratch out 'Benny's' eyes if she had claws!" William had told me once long ago, and we both had shrieked with laughter at the joke.

But it wasn't funny at all.

In cold, stark reality, when you were only six years old, the Dragon's claws were frightening and fearful.

"A few more of your 'tender little lambs,' I presume?" asked our new teacher with a leering smile. "Thank you, Miss Bennett. You may safely leave them with me. I'm not a wolf, you know, and I shan't devour them!"

"Ha! ha! ha! Ha! ha! ha!"

A strange mechanical laughter echoed around the classroom and stopped so abruptly it seemed that the Dragon had demanded the children to laugh at her jokes—yet she hadn't even turned her head.

Miss Bennett gave each of us in turn a long, lingering glance and went back to the Infants' School, closing the door softly behind her—forever.

We filed quietly and obediently on to the front form and sat down. We all were sniffing and sniveling, even the boys, and we stared hypnotized through a blur of tears at the face of our new teacher.

She stared back, and her eyes held the same unwavering magnetism as a cat watching a mouse.

Her mouth was thin and cruel. Her hair was cropped short like a man's, and she wore a black tailored costume with a collared blouse and tie.

Her plainness was emphasized by the severity of her dress—Miss Bennett always wore soft pastel shades, and her hair in a bun.

At last, when we all fully understood the awful implications of those pale hypnotic eyes, she went on with the interrupted lesson and left us alone for the rest of the afternoon, "to finish our sniffing and sniveling"—and to get more and more uncomfortable, wanting to be "excused."

"*You* ask, Evelyn," I whispered imploringly.

"No, *you*." She was a year older than the rest of us, but all her superiority had collapsed like a pricked balloon.

So we sat fretting and fidgeting and nudging each other.

"You ask." . . . "No, you."

35

Suddenly the Dragon raised her hand, and the whole class stopped their monotonous chanting: "Twice three is six . . . twice four is eight."

"I observe a slight disturbance among our new pupils in the front row," we heard her say meaningly. "*You!* Stand up!"

I blinked stupidly and remained seated till Evelyn, happily spared this ordeal, gave me a push, and I stood up trembling like a leaf in the wind.

"What is your name?"

"Sarah Shears."

"Sarah Shears, Teacher."

"Sarah Shears—Teacher."

"How old are you, Sarah Shears?"

"Six—Teacher."

"So, you are six years old, and I suppose you think you are a very clever little girl? Oh, come, come! No need to be shy, no need to be modest. We all know what a clever little girl you are, don't we, children?"

"Yes, Teacher!" they chorused.

Tears filled my eyes and spilled slowly down my hot cheeks.

"Perhaps you can tell me, Sarah Shears, since you are so clever, what all the whispering is about?"

I gulped. "P-p-please, Teacher, we want to be excused."

She glanced along the row of pleading tear-smudged faces, but there was no pity in those pale eyes, only contempt.

"I'll think about it," she decided and went on with the lesson—"Twice five is ten . . . twice six is twelve" —till a wail of shame and dismay ("I've done it!" from Emily) halted the chanting voices of the children once again.

"You have my permission to leave the room," ordered our new teacher. "Emily Mason, you may go home."

I soon noticed the Dragon had her special pets—all boys on the back row, and ready for Standard Two. Although she tormented the boys, she didn't persecute them as she did the girls and the new children from the Infants'. William, I remember, had rather enjoyed his daily encounter with the Dragon. But William was bold and brave, and afraid of nothing and nobody!

In this strange new environment we wilted, like flowers without the sun. Only the bullies in the back row, and the fortunate few who could make their minds a blank, suffered no lasting ill effect from the Dragon's claws. She had her own peculiar system of instruction that included not only reading, writing, and arithmetic (known as the "3 R's") but also lessons of her own clever invention, with such titles as "What I Had for Breakfast."

"What does Mother wear?"

"What does Father write in his letters?"

"What kind of furniture do you have in your bedroom?"

"What did you say to the Vicar when he called?"— and others of equal personal significance.

I enjoyed the reading, writing, and arithmetic but disliked and distrusted the rest of her curriculum.

Standing stiff as a ramrod beside her blackboard, she would call on certain children at random, one by one, to join her in front of the class—to answer the particular question she had chosen as her "subject" and then to write it legibly with white chalk on the blackboard. Conspicuous in the front row, I could never hide from her darting eyes, and when her glance fell on me, I shrank into a kind of stupor and was completely dumb.

One day during our first week in Standard One, we were faced with the question "What did I have for breakfast?"

Hoots of laughter followed poor stupid Freda Osborne, who scrawled PORIG in large sprawling letters on the blackboard, then giggled helplessly and ran back to her seat.

Scholar followed scholar, but none could spell what they had for breakfast, so it made a lot of fun, for teacher and the big boys, but only added to the misery of the shy little girls still awaiting their turn.

The suspense was terrible, for you never knew when your turn would come or whether you would escape. But there was no escape for me that day.

"You! Sarah Shears, stand up and come forward!"

I shivered with an icy chill, but my face was burning hot. I opened my mouth to speak, but no words came; an invisible cord had tied my tongue.

"Well, Sarah Shears? We are waiting."

The heavy silence was broken only by the nervous sniffing of Emily, who had not yet recovered from her shameful ordeal of that first day.

"Well, our clever little scholar from the Infants' seems to have lost her tongue."

The boys hooted and the girls giggled, while Evelyn, watching my red contorted face, began to cry in sympathy. The Dragon shrugged her thin shoulders, handed me the chalk, and suggested I might like to write it, since, like Zachariah, I was obviously struck dumb.

With a trembling hand I wrote in bold capitals, BREAD LARD SUGAR.

The boys on the back row were tickled to death.

"Lard!" they groaned, slapping each other on the back. "Can you believe it—Sarah Shears has lard on her bread!"

Teacher raised her hand and the pandemonium ceased. Then she looked down at me with fresh interest.

"Haven't you make a mistake, Sarah Shears? Don't you mean margarine, not lard?" (She pronounced "margarine" with a hard "g," but Mother, who was a good scholar, pronounced it with a soft "g.")

I shook my head and vainly tried to speak, while the children stared, fascinated by my sudden dumbness, and I struggled not to cry.

At last a word came tumbling out, followed by others. "P-p-please, Teacher, we had lard on our b-b-bread."

More titters from the class, for this was much more fun than "Twice three is six, twice four is eight"—and Sarah Shears was actually stuttering.

Teacher raised her eyebrows.

"So, you have lard on your bread for breakfast, and not margarine, and sprinkled with sugar, no doubt?"

I nodded vigorously, because speech was so difficult.

"Sarah Shears actually likes lard on her bread. In fact she prefers it to margarine," she told the class. "Let us hope it will give her the strength to speak up properly next time. Class dismissed!"

Mother had bought a few hens and a cock from one of the neighbors and contrived to build a henhouse in the back yard from the tumbling remains of an old shed, a few yards of rusty wire netting, and a broken clothes prop.

The hens were brown and scraggy, the cock sleek

A Village Girl

and handsome, with a glaring eye and magnificent blood-red comb. He had an arrogant, strutting walk.

The first morning in their new home, the cock crowed so loudly at daybreak that we all were alarmed and rushed downstairs in our nightgowns.

"Goodness gracious me!" Mother exclaimed, as surprised as we were by this sudden commotion in the back yard.

"Perhaps it's hungry?" William suggested, rubbing the sleep from his eyes. "Let's give it some corn." And he ran out with a handful of yellow maize.

The cock devoured it greedily and looked for more, while the little brown hens stood watching politely.

"I don't like him. He's greedy," I decided, and went back to bed.

William came slowly back upstairs, chewing maize, and he threw me a piece in passing. I chewed and chewed, but found it dull and tasteless, so I spat it out under the bed.

Mother had a very good reason for buying the cock and the hens, as she had a very good reason for everything, and it was not a sudden whim. The war dragged on, rationing became erratic, food was scarce, especially dairy foods, and we children must have eggs. Mother had profound faith in the rich nourishment of eggs for growing children, and her huge delight in the first brown egg she found in the straw one morning was so infectious we all gathered around to inspect it and to exclaim about its color, size, and shape.

"Tomorrow I hope there will be another, so we will wait and see, then perhaps you can all have eggs for dinner!" Mother declared, and she looked so pleased I gave her a hug and went off to school singing "The Farmer's Boy."

The little brown hen "obliged" again the second day—the others were still too young to lay eggs, Mother thought. But the egg dinner was messy and disappointing. Spread on several thick slices of bread and margarine, with the yellow evenly mixed with the white— which we all disliked—I thought I should be sick, and even Mary spat it out.

"Two eggs between four of us?" asked William scornfully. "No, thanks!" And he pushed it away.

Mother was annoyed and very disappointed.

"Ungrateful children, you deserve to *starve*," she told us severely.

Then she scooped it off the bread and fed it to Henry, who ate simply everything!

Mother brought us up on some very fine principles and a few wise proverbs, including:

Waste not, want not.
Never put off till tomorrow what you should do today.
Many hands make light work.
If at first you don't succeed, try again.
Cut your coat according to your cloth.
A fool and his money are soon parted.
Penny wise, pound foolish.
A rolling stone gathers no moss.

The last of these proverbs was probably a hint to Father, though I failed to understand its proper implication. Who wants to gather moss, anyway?

As children, we were constantly reminded of these wise old proverbs handed down from generation to generation until it came to our turn to hear them.

41

There were other proverbs, too, that flatly contradicted the few Mother expounded.

For instance, "Too many cooks spoil the broth" was no substitute for "Many hands make light work" in her opinion.

As for "Make hay while the sun shines," she had no patience with that one either, for it had a hidden meaning, she explained, that had nothing to do with hay, but only pleasure and profit. So we were advised to forget it and to remember only such wise proverbs as "Penny wise, pound foolish" or "A fool and his money are soon parted." Her regular day-by-day proverb was, however, "If at first you don't succeed, try again."

And one or all of us (for even young Henry was included in this theory) were reminded, quietly but firmly, we could expect no help from Mother until we had tried again—and yet again!

To admit defeat seemed to Mother the one inexcusable fault, for she herself was one of the Undefeated. Undefeated by changing circumstance, by war, by constant separation from her husband, by near poverty, by frozen pipes and flooded closets, by her son's flaming temper or her daughter's tears!

To Mother we looked for the truth in all things, for guidance and strength. To Mother we ran for comfort. To Mother I prayed every night as a little girl, and not to God, for I needed a God I could touch and see. Mother was God, and I worshiped her. She was so dependable, so strong, so secure, and her word was law. We had no real need for a father, we children decided, as the weeks and months and years went by without a man in the house.

But who can tell what Mother needed? Were her

children really sufficient for her strong maternal nature, or did she long for a husband and lover, like other women?

We shall never know, for she did not speak her private thoughts to anyone, not even to her best beloved first-born son. She had strange reserve, our mother, and her secret thoughts were too far removed from our daily intercourse to probe. If Father also dwelt in this small secret place in her heart, she kept it secret and never disclosed it to us as children. She still insisted, however, that Father was the head of the family.

Loyalty was demanded, and respect, for this far-distant figure whose face was already a blurred image and whose voice was completely forgotten. She tried so hard to keep his memory alive, especially for the younger children, and William supported her strongly in this matter.

"Don't forget now, your father is a Regimental Sergeant Major, and he's so strong he could kill all those beastly Turks with his bare hands!"

This, I felt, was going a little too far.

Mary and Henry had no recollections at all of Father—only a photograph in a silver frame they obediently kissed good night.

"Your father would be proud of you" was praise indeed, but was it not important that Mother should be proud, too?

"Your father likes the table laid properly, Sarah," she would remind me when I forgot the forks for our pudding, or the four tablespoons were jumbled in a heap and not tidily arranged in pairs on either side of the cruet.

"But we don't use four tablespoons ever, and it's

such a waste," I would complain, but Mother was adamant.

All the little brown hens were laying eggs at last, so we hadn't to make do with two eggs between four of us, but had one each for dinner twice a week.

Meat was scarce and expensive, and fish, apart from dried haddock, we had not seen for months.

"All the fishermen have gone to war, silly!" was William's brief explanation when I ventured to inquire why we had nothing but dried haddock.

Mother was determined, however, to feed her brood, no matter what the Kaiser said about "starving us out."

"Ridiculous! Who does he think he is, anyway?" she would exclaim indignantly, after scanning the pages of the *Daily News*. Then she would proceed to the Depot in the village with a large stone jar tucked in the well of the pram to queue for black treacle!

"Golden syrup," that relish of prewar days, had disappeared altogether—and so had strawberry jam. But Mother insisted that black treacle was much more nutritious for growing children because it was so pure—and she poured it liberally over our suet pudding.

"But I don't like black treacle!" I wailed. "It makes me feel sick."

"Then be sick, for goodness' sake!" said Mother tartly, feeding Henry a large spoonful.

She also discovered she could grow enormous marrows on the rubbish heap in the back yard, because potatoes were also scarce; so we had to make do with boiled marrow twice a week. It was a wet, insipid substitute for potatoes, and such refinements as white sauce were unknown to Mother. She never disguised anything, for this would be "pampering," in her opinion.

"There are plenty of poor starving children who would be glad to eat it" was her prompt answer to any complaint. I sometimes wished the starving children would take my share.

The marrows were also useful for jam-making, we were told, since marrow required only a small quantity of preserving sugar, plus a few chunks of preserved ginger left over from a previous Christmas.

So Mother went off again to the Depot to queue for preserving sugar. But the jam refused to jell and it still tasted like marrow.

Why wouldn't it jell? Mother had followed the recipe in the cookery book most carefully—so she said.

Marrow jam on our bread and margarine at tea-time turned out to be even more unpleasant than black treacle on our suet pudding!

The kindly neighbors, who had large gardens, then arrived with their arms piled with rhubarb—also for jam. Mother was so delighted with this further supply that she went off immediately to the Depot for more sugar. Since this extra ration of preserving sugar was allowed only for jam, she took the precaution of presenting the "kind ladies of the Depot" with a jar of her homemade marrow jam!

But the rhubarb wouldn't jell either. It was poured over bread like stewed rhubarb, and we all complained bitterly about the mess. Still mother refused to admit defeat.

"It's a particular kind of rhubarb, and it's not supposed to be set," she explained, feeding Henry again with a large spoonful. "Henry likes it, and *I* like it!"

These were her final words on the question of whether or not the jam should jell—and we knew it!

Monday always being "washing day," we had to make do with a quickly prepared dinner, so Monday held no surprises, ever. Cold meat left over from Sunday's meager joint, if we had a joint, but often only pudding, which Mother called "hasty dumplings"—for hasty they were!

At five to twelve—with the big copper boiling and bubbling over with the week's family wash, and steam filling the kitchen—Mother would hurriedly dry her hands and mix together a little flour, lard, and water with a large pinch of salt—to give the dumplings a nutty flavor. Rolled into balls, she dropped them quickly into a large pot of boiling water, where they swelled and swelled enormously.

They quickly subsided, however, on our plates, and the inevitable black treacle was poured over. William actually enjoyed these hasty dumplings and usually ate three.

A tiny packet of butter weighing only a quarter of a pound was our ration for the week, together with margarine and lard. Mother kept the precious little morsel to herself. It was her only luxury and she richly deserved it.

Once upon a time, a scraggy little brown hen, incapable of laying any more eggs, was killed and plucked (by a neighbor who had a stomach for such things). Mother then roasted it for Sunday dinner to give us all a nice surprise.

Even William was disgusted at such barbarism. "It's wicked! It's cruel!" he told Mother in a flaming temper when he discovered the source of the savory aroma after attending Sunday School.

"It's not chicken—it's poor little Betsy Ann!" I

sobbed, shuddering as the sharp knife stabbed her breast.

"Poor Mother, not poor Betsy Ann," she retorted smartly. "Sarah, go upstairs to bed—at once!"

"I'm going to bed, too," William told her defiantly. "I'm not eating *her!*"

Since I started school, I was given pocket money—a penny a week, regularly—every Saturday morning. William now received threepence.

"What do I get when I'm ten?" he demanded, for threepence was not nearly enough to cover his mounting hobbies and expenses.

"When you are ten, William, you will get sixpence a week pocket money," Mother told him promptly.

"Gosh!" exclaimed William, shiny-eyed with expectation. "I can hardly wait!"

Mother also saved all the farthings for the little ones so they too could share in the Saturday morning orgy. She often received a farthing change from the milkman and baker, and such small articles as cotton, tape, hat elastic, linen buttons, and mending wools were all priced at a penny and three farthings.

So, with my own shining new penny I also took four farthings to buy Mary and Henry each an ounce of chocolate drops. Since I started school, I was also considered capable of taking Mary with me on this short Saturday morning excursion to Mrs. Mercer's sweetshop.

Mother would wave us off and watch our slow progress a little anxiously, because of the danger of passing horses, farm wagons, and flocks of sheep, which blocked the road so completely we had to crouch under a hedge until they had passed by.

Mary was still a tiny doll-like creature, with pretty

curly hair and perfect features. She had the tiniest hands and feet, and weighed much less than Henry, who was two years younger. Her smile was shy and sweet, and she was always good, her demands being few—an old rag doll to cuddle, Mother within sight, and her big sister Sarah not too far away. Mother had warned us to be gentle with Mary, for she hadn't our sturdy independence and would always need a lot of care and protection. Even William was gentle with Mary, but boisterously rough with young Henry.

On Saturday mornings, however, Mary was completely my responsibility, for William disappeared into the fields and woods and only came home when he was hungry. With her tiny hand trustfully in mine, I felt her need for care and protection most acutely, and stopped every few yards to smother her with hugs and kisses. But she was easily frightened, and the short journey became quite perilous when the Gentry rode past on their prancing horses, flourishing riding crops and shouting arrogantly to each other.

Flattened against the churchyard wall, I would press Mary's terrified face to my pinafore and enfold her trembling little body in my arms.

"Beasts! Rude beasts! I hate you all!" I would cry after them, but my thin piping voice would be lost in the clatter of hoofs and rattle of stirrups.

Sometimes they would condescend to notice us, like two little dogs in the gutter, and one of the Young Gentlemen would wave his riding crop and call out, "Hello, little girls! Do we frighten you?"—then laugh jeeringly at our discomfort. Mother was much too proud to call them the "Gentry" and gave them all their proper names. Neither did she address anyone as "sir" or "madam." We lived in a cottage, but Mother was never a "cottager."

Mrs. Mercer's sweetshop had a low counter filled with the most exciting assortment of sweets in cardboard boxes.

Mrs. Mercer was old and crippled with rheumatism. She was quite alone in the world, so her customers, especially the children, not only gave her a meager living but provided constant pleasure. Her thin, wispy hair barely covered her head, and her pink scalp, as she bent over the counter, was quite fascinating to a child accustomed to a family with rich, abundant hair.

Mrs. Mercer never hurried, no matter what the time of day, and she had all the time in the world to attend to her customers.

"Good morning, Mrs. Mercer," I would begin politely, with an eye on the big striped humbugs.

"Good morning, my dear, and how are you today?" Mrs. Mercer would reply with equal politeness.

"Quite well, thank you," I answered mechanically.

Then we got down to business.

It was Mary's privilege to choose first, but her choice never varied, and her finger pointed always to the same box: "Packer's chocolate drops, ½d. an ounce" or two farthings would do.

"And another ounce for the baby." Mrs. Mercer carefully weighed them on her scales and popped them into two separate bags, to be proudly carried home by Mary.

I handed over the four farthings. Now it was my turn to choose. Would it be something to chew or something to crunch? Something savory, or something sickly sweet? Would it be aniseed balls, to last all day and

change color every five minutes, or a big striped hum-
bug, strong with peppermint?

"It's so difficult, Mrs. Mercer," I sighed.

"I know, dear, but take your time."

She sat down to wait patiently on her high stool.
So I shut my eyes, counted "eeny, meeny, miney, mo,"
and jabbed. It was aniseed balls, and twelve a penny!

Mrs. Mercer carefully counted them out in assorted
colors and we both exchanged another smile of complete understanding as she opened the door for me.

"Thank you, my dear. Goodbye till next Saturday."

The bell clanged in her little parlor, and we caught
a glimpse of a crackling wood fire and a cat curled on
the hearthrug.

The journey back was almost at a trot, for we could
hardly wait to start on the sweets we had bought.

Mother's ruling was firm, however, and we dared
not disobey. "Only poor children eat in the street."

Henry, in Mother's arms, at the window, would
open his mouth wide like a young bird in the nest, and
Mary would carefully pop in a chocolate drop. Then we
handed the bags to Mother, who took one sweet from
each, though we seldom saw her eating them. The remainder we kept—to eat or save or share between us,
exactly as we pleased. While Mary sat quietly down on
the kitchen floor with the bag on her lap, I ran upstairs
to curl up on the wide windowsill of the bedroom I
shared with Mary, with a book on my knees and an
aniseed ball rolling slowly around my tongue.

This was my idea of Heaven—a quiet corner, a
book, and an aniseed ball!

"I've g-g-got another s-s-stomachache," I told
Mother when she insisted that I eat up my porridge like

a good girl and take a brisk run with my hoop before school. It was Monday morning again, and washing day—a most inconvenient time to have a stomachache.

Mother sighed as she knelt on the cold stone floor to light the copper fire with a bundle of dry sticks we had gathered on Saturday.

"Why must you always have your stomachache on Monday, Sarah?" she complained.

"I d-d-don't know. I c-c-can't help it if it c-c-comes on M-M-Monday. I'm s-s-sorry, Mother."

I stood there hugging my stomach and miserably aware of her displeasure.

"You are sure it's not an excuse to get out of a particular lesson you dislike?"

"No, Mother."

"But you don't enjoy going to school any more?" I shook my head sadly. "Why don't you like school, Sarah?"

"I d-d-don't know."

"But you must know," she insisted. "*Why* don't you like school, Sarah? And why are you stuttering? You used not to stutter in the Infants' School—only since you've been moved up to Standard One. Well, someone in that class is turning you into a nervous wreck, my child, and I won't have it. Is it Miss Drake?"

I shook my head vigorously, for wild horses would not drag it out of me. Mother would put on her hat and gloves and march out to see the Headmaster, leaving me to mind Mary and Henry and the copper. This I knew, for it had happened once before, when William was in trouble at school.

He came home one day holding both ears and almost in tears with the pain.

"I will not have my children's ears boxed!" Mother

51

declared, her eyes flashing with angry determination. "Smack their bottoms, or cane their hands, yes, certainly, if punishment is deserved. But boxing children's ears is highly dangerous! Sit down, William, and eat your dinner. Sarah, mind the little ones. I am going straight to the Headmaster."

"I don't want any dinner, it hurts," William complained, crouching over the fire.

"Then I'll make you some nice hot cocoa," said Mother comfortingly.

The interview with the Headmaster that day was not discussed with her children on her return.

"But what did you say?" William demanded. "I want to know."

"Never mind what I said, it was strictly confidential," she told him firmly. But we never had our ears boxed again.

Yet I was afraid to tell her about the Dragon's persecution, because I knew Mother would go to the Headmaster again to complain, and I should suffer even more from her sarcasm, and sarcasm was horrid because it was so polite.

"I could lie on the sofa in the front room? I won't be a nuisance, Mother, I promise."

"All right, go and lie down, and when the fire is well alight, I'll get you the hot-water bottle."

"Thank you," I breathed gratefully.

We had only one stone bottle to be shared by all the family—"when you felt poorly." Wrapped in an old flannel petticoat of Henry's, it was warm and comforting.

"Here you are, Sarah. Now lie still and keep warm, and you will soon feel better," said Mother briskly ten minutes later. She tucked me up with the hot bottle under a blanket, dropped a kiss on my brow, and went back to the washtub. Dear Mother! How I loved her!

The relief was so great, I cried softly and silently into the cushion for some time, till the pain subsided into a dull ache, and I slept till dinnertime.

"Can you eat a dumpling, Sarah?" called Mother from the kitchen.

"No, thank you." I shuddered under the blanket and patted my poor sick stomach.

I could smell the horrid smell of boiling clothes in the copper and hear William demanding more black treacle.

When he had finished his dinner, he put his head around the door, grinned amiably, and said, "I told the Dragon you were sick, and she said to tell you she was sorry and she hoped you would soon be better."

We smiled at each other complacently, for we both knew she didn't mean it.

"William," I whispered, "I should like some bread and milk."

It was his turn to shudder now, for he loathed bread and milk.

"I'll tell Mother. 'Bye!" He was gone.

Some time later, Mother came in with Mary and Henry, and the bread and milk. They stood in a row, looking down anxiously at my peaked face, while I emptied the small basin.

Then Mary ran back to fetch her treasured rag doll, and Henry gave me a kiss.

"Have you still got a bad stomachache, or only a little one?" Mother wanted to know.

"Only a little one," I confessed.

53

She sighed with relief, for she hadn't to call in Dr. Bird and pay his enormous fee (seven and sixpence). "Let me look at it."

Her hard work-roughened hand prodded my stomach, and I winced with pain.

"I can't understand it. You begin to look like a pickaninny, Sarah, with this large protruding stomach, and the rest of you so small and skinny. But perhaps you will grow to it?" she decided hopefully as she tucked me up again for the afternoon.

"Would you like a book?"

"Can I have 'The Snow Goose'?"

"Yes, Mary will fetch it for you."

But soon I was asleep again, till the clatter of tea-cups woke me at four o'clock. When they all trooped in with a nice cup of tea and a small sponge cake, the pain had gone, and I was ready to get up for a game of Ludo.

Mother had instituted a Children's Hour from five to six o'clock every evening, when she played quiet games with us and helped us with spelling and sums. She also taught me to sew and knit, and encouraged William with his collection of pressed flowers.

We sat together in the lamplight, with Henry on Mother's lap, and it was so peaceful and pleasant, after the stomachache, with washing day over for another week, Mother relaxed and gentle, and even William forgetting to be bossy, most agreeably kind.

The Children's Hour was my solace and salvation, after the hazards of Standard One, and as regular as our dose of Syrup-of-Figs.

3
Tapioca for Tea

Spring came early to our lovely vale of Kent. It came with the first soft southerly breeze, the first primroses, the first lamb, and the first green hawthorn buds, crisp and sweet to eat. We called it "bread and cheese." Perched on the hill, we looked down into this green fertile valley from wide-flung windows, breathing the breath of spring in small ecstatic gasps of pleasure and surprise. Each one of us, suddenly released from a long winter of snow and sleet, damp and drafts, and wet, uncomfortable clothes, stretched and yawned in the warm spring sunshine, and smiled.

Mother smiled because she could start on the spring cleaning, and already her active mind was tackling the job with fresh energy and enthusiasm. A bucket of whitewash for kitchen walls and ceiling stood ready for use on top of the copper.

She would wash all the curtains, covers, and counterpanes, air all the mattresses, and beat all the mats.

She would turn out drawers and cupboards but put everything back—for it "might come in useful someday."

For Mother, the first soft breath of spring brought no lingering desire to wander afield in search of periwinkles and primroses, or just to stand and dream. Her urgent desire was simply for a clean and shining house, and the smell of fresh paint and furniture polish was far more pleasing to her than the faint elusive scent of a primrose.

William whooped with a wild delight—tossing his overcoat, gloves, and scarf in the air, where they fell unheeded to the floor and were picked up later by Sarah.

"Ne'er cast a clout till May is out!" Mother called after him as he darted away, swift as a swallow. His cheeky laughter floated back on the warm southern breeze, and Mother smiled at his daring and was not angry. She stood for a long moment watching the small sturdy figure climb easily up and over the five-barred gate and run swiftly across the field.

When he disappeared through a gap in the hedge, she was still smiling whimsically. "Boys will be boys" was all she said, and with all my heart I wished I was a boy!

Girls may also feel the same wild urge to fling their clothes in the air, but girls must conquer the urge and behave nicely. Girls must learn to wait, as their mothers waited, for something to happen, and not go in search of it. They could have their daydreams, but "duty" often prevented any realization of those dreams.

This compelling urge to run from house and home,

to taste the sweet intoxication of freedom, to look and linger, peer and ponder, was not for girls. (Oh, Mother, *please* let me go!)

"What did you say, Sarah?" she asked sharply.

"Nothing."

She looked at me suspiciously.

"We must take the little ones for a nice walk on Sunday afternoon."

"Yes, Mother."

"Come along now. You can't stop all day staring out of the window. I want you to run to the grocer to get me some more Robin's Starch. Henry could start wearing William's white sailor suit at Easter. Then you could help me to strip off the beds and polish the brass doorknobs. Run along now like a good girl, and stop pouting, it's ugly."

"I don't care."

"Don't answer me back, Sarah!"

"Sorry, Mother."

She gave me threepence for the starch and told me to hurry.

"C-c-can I go without my s-s-scarf?"

"Yes, all right, but hurry."

"And my gloves?"

"Goodness gracious me, child, you would try the patience of a saint. Yes, you may leave off your scarf and gloves, but nothing more."

Mary was sitting quietly on the front doorstep nursing her doll. She seemed a little anxious that the door might close behind her, shutting her off from all the familiar sounds and smells in the kitchen, and Mother's voice, so I told Henry to sit on the hassock and prop the door open, then I had to find him something to play with, or he wouldn't stay. "Are you still there, Sarah?" called Mother from a bedroom window, but I pretended not to hear.

Mary and Henry, still wrapped in all their winter clothes, had no recollection of other spring days, but they turned their smiling faces to the sun instinctively.

As I went away, Henry snatched off his woolly hat and threw it in the road.

"Oh, Henry! That's naughty," I told him severely, for I saw the beginning of another William.

"Boys will be boys," said Mother complacently on her way to the washtub, her arms piled high with dirty curtains, covers, and counterpanes.

"It's not fair!" I grumbled as I went on my way to the grocer's.

Halfway down the village street I remembered and stopped, sucking in my breath nervously. I was going to stutter. Starch began with "s," and "s" was one of my worst letters, together with "b," "c," "m," "p," and "t." These six letters of the alphabet were tied to my tongue by this invisible cord. Why did it have to be starch? Why not haricot beans, lemons, or rice? All these words I could manage to say without any difficulty. Why hadn't I asked Mother to write it down?

Because she would have refused to do so. It was a good "memory test," she would say, and only six or more articles were written down.

Should I buy a lemon *and* starch? With threepence? No, quite impossible. Perhaps if I went on a detour through the village, instead of taking my usual short cut, I should have more time to prepare myself for Mr. Green's brisk "Well, Sarah, and what can I do for you?" Humming a cheerful hymn might also help.

So I dawdled slowly through the village and passed

the shop twice, still humming my favorite hymn—"All Things Bright and Beautiful."

My next favorites—"Away in a Manger" and "Fight the Good Fight"—hadn't quite the same effect, so I kept to the first, hopefully.

But it didn't work, and I knew it hadn't worked.

Why could I sing and not talk without stuttering? What was the matter with me? Should I never be able to talk as I talked in Infants' School, easily and effortlessly? Would grownups always stare uncomfortably and children titter, always, for the rest of my life? This appalling thought brought tears of self-pity to my eyes, and my throat was parched and tight.

Hot with shame and panic, I saw Mrs. Croucher approaching the shop with a large shopping basket, and Mr. Green, standing behind the counter, actually waiting for a customer.

This was my best moment of the day. Now, I told myself decisively. But already it was too late, and Mrs. Croucher pushed past me and went in. "Hello, Sarah—shopping?" she asked curiously. I nodded, dumb with dismay, for now I had to wait till she came out, and I knew she liked a good gossip with the grocer.

Still clutching my threepence, I started to rehearse. *Starch—starch—starch.* But of *course* I could say "starch" without stuttering! It was easy, wasn't it! I had only to take a deep breath, walk boldly up to the counter, and say "Starch"! What a silly little goose! Ha! ha! I grinned back at my reflection in the window. Mother was right, of course. She was always right.

"If at first you don't succeed, *try again.*"

Mrs. Croucher was already packing the groceries into her basket and preparing to leave.

Now, on the count of three—no, six—no, ten—on

the count of ten, I go in. I began to count slowly, taking a deep breath between each count to make it longer.

Mrs. Croucher would think it was a little odd, surely, to find me still staring fixedly at the window when she came out.

She would peer at me suspiciously, for she was always suspicious of everyone (since her daughter ran off with a Canadian lumberjack).

So I had to get inside the shop before she came out. That was obvious. No more excuses, no more humming —all things were not bright and beautiful, anyway— no more counting up to ten, and no more grinning in the shop window, I decided.

Sarah Shears! *Open the door and walk straight in! Go on! Now!*

I suddenly found myself inside, and Mrs. Croucher on the way out.

"*Starch*," I called out loudly and urgently before I even reached the counter, and Mrs. Croucher jumped in the air with surprise, muttered, "Manners—kids these days ain't got no manners," and went out.

It was out! Oh, the glow of pride and achievement!

Mr. Green's smiling benevolent face leaned over to ask, "Did you say starch, Sarah?" My face flushed, and a cold shiver ran down my spine.

Please, please, God, don't let him ask me to repeat it. I should die! I thought. But he didn't. I ran all the way home and tumbled in the door panting.

"And about time, too," said Mother tartly. "I was just coming to search for you."

Sunday was my favorite day of the week. We started to prepare for it early Saturday evening, as soon as Mother's Children's Hour was over.

As Monday was always washing day, so Saturday was always bath night. It hardly varied throughout our childhood. To be suddenly told to take a bath on Wednesday would be unthinkable, and quite impossible.

Once again, Mother struggled to light the obstinate copper fire, and as the steam rose in clouds from the broken copper lid, we began to make our own separate preparations for the bath—starting with Henry and working through to William by about eight o'clock. William was seldom ready and always reluctant to take a bath, pretending he hadn't sufficient warning, or he felt "queer." This "queerness" was quickly recognized by Mother as nothing more serious than "bath escapism," so she ignored William's groans and grumbles, while she vigorously lathered young Henry. The big zinc bath, drawn in front of a roaring fire, was long and deep, and as comfortable as it was possible to be in our drafty kitchen.

No time was allowed for playing and splashing, and toy ducks were definitely taboo. It was a major operation, and treated as such. The little ones had Pear's soap, and the rest carbolic. On the very day you started school you started also on the carbolic.

"Sarah, get your head out of that book and help Mary to undress," Mother would remind me sharply, with Henry already seated on a warm towel, being vigorously rubbed dry.

Mary stood obediently on the hassock while I stripped off her clothes, and she shivered a little in her nakedness.

"Now sit on the hassock and rub Henry's hair dry," said Mother.

Clean and sweet-smelling, he was dumped on my lap.

A Village Girl

His pink cheeks, glowing from Mother's brisk rubbing, felt warm and soft against my face. His shining fair hair, still damp from the bath, had no curling tendencies like the rest of us but lay sleek and flat to his head like a cap of gold.

He was a lovable little boy, now that he had stopped that awful screaming for attention, and he played quite happily most of the day, with oddments of wood, a few colored bricks, and anything that William could spare from his own private collection.

(It was a golden rule that we ask permission before taking each other's private possessions.)

With Henry's fat little arms entwined around my neck, I struggled to dry his hair. But already he had started to tease Mary, as William teased me, and, leaning over the bath, he tickled the back of her neck and splashed a handful of soapsuds over her short curly hair.

They smiled at each other with complete understanding. They seemed much quieter and more content than William and I had been at this age. Not so curious by nature, or so eager to explore beyond the boundaries of the cottage. They both were essentially "Mother's children" and only unhappy when she was out of sight.

But nobody could ever say we were "like four little peas in a pod"—as they said of the Partridge children— for we all were different and distinct, not only in feature but in character and temperament.

This extraordinary difference in brothers and sisters surprised not only the neighbors but Mother herself, and she was constantly looking for some small resemblance. I copied some of William's habits and mannerisms, as Mary copied mine, and Henry copied Mary, but that was all.

This surprising individualism grew more pronounced as we grew older and ceased to copy anything from each other, yet always we felt a keen awareness of each other's place in the family, and its completeness, when we were together. Each in turn defended the younger with fierce protectiveness. That William bossed and bullied me at home, but promptly beat up any other boy who only pulled my hair, was not considered odd or unusual.

Every Saturday night, on the chair beside each bed, our Sunday clothes were laid out ready in neat little piles, with freshly polished Sunday shoes underneath.

To Mary clung a faint fragrance of Pear's soap as she climbed into bed, with her damp curls making a halo around her small face. I climbed in beside her, smelling strongly of carbolic, with my hair in curling rags. All my life, the smell of carbolic would remind me of that large masculine district nurse in a starched apron, prodding my head with two sharp knitting needles!

Sunday morning dawned pleasantly, and most surprisingly, with Mother bringing mugs of tea to everyone in bed! Sunday School, at ten o'clock, left ample time for leisurely dressing and breakfast.

William would grunt and grumble at being disturbed with a mug of tea, but grumble still more if he was not included.

Then, in less than five minutes, he would be asleep again.

Henry, always the first to wake, and chirpy as a sparrow, would demand to get up and go downstairs.

Mary and I, flat on our stomachs, with a book on the pillow, prepared for a quiet half-hour of Sunday reading. *Andersen's Fairy Tales*, *Mother Goose*, or the

Bible were my own particular favorites now, but Mary had no preference and seemed to enjoy them all equally. She let me read without interruption and completely overlooked my stuttering, so I often found myself quite surprisingly fluent.

"Just sponge your hands and faces only, since you had a bath last night," said Mother as she carefully dressed young Henry in the white sailor suit that once upon a time had belonged to William.

Sunday was the only day in the week when William was obliged to conform to certain standards of dress and behavior. This put him in a bad mood right from the start, and he disliked Sundays as heartily as I liked them.

We set off for Sunday School, holding Mary's hand while Mother watched proudly from the doorstep and Henry demanding to join us.

But Mother was adamant. Henry was still too young, and she would take him to church later, where we would join her in a back pew, convenient for sneaking out before the sermon—never less than half an hour, and very tedious.

"Six days shalt thou labor, but the seventh day is the Sabbath," we were constantly reminded as children.

You did not therefore expect a hot roast dinner or potatoes without their jackets. The only luxury allowed was a fruit pie, baked on Saturday and warmed in the oven.

Draped in bibs and pinafores to cover our Sunday clothes, we sat stiffly and uncomfortably around the front-room table, longing for the comfortable ease of the kitchen.

William, resplendent in his first suit, with a starched white napkin under his chin to mark his superiority, remarked gloomily, "I suppose we have to take a walk."

"Yes, William." Mother was firmly decided on this matter and would listen to no excuses. "All the winter, you have been allowed to go to bed with a book on Sunday afternoons, but now the winter is over, and we all need to get out in the fresh air for a nice walk."

"I hate walks," argued William. "I get tired."

"Oh, William! And you walk for miles on Saturday and never complain?"

"That's not walking—that's mooching," he reminded her.

"Well, you are jolly lucky, William. I can't ever mooch," I told him—and he promptly told me to shut up!

"William! what would your father say? Such language! And Sunday, too!" Mother was appalled.

"Say 'sorry,' " Mary suggested sweetly, smiling at his gloomy face.

"Sorry," said William obligingly, kicking the table leg.

So we went for our Sunday walk resplendent in our Sunday clothes, and our Sunday behavior was almost impeccable.

But I was a girl, and already dress-conscious, so I enjoyed the nice remarks that people made about our appearance—and Mary enjoyed it too. We strutted along like two little peacocks, tossing our curls and swinging white-gloved hands, while William strolled nonchalantly behind.

"Your father will be home soon, and he will expect you to behave like well-bred children."

"Your father will be home soon, and he will expect you to eat up everything on your plates."

"Your father will be home soon, and he will expect you to wait on me, not me to wait on you."

These threats were getting more and more frequent of late, and we began to wish all over again that Father would stay in that mysterious place with the funny name—Mesopotamia—forever. We were perfectly content with Mother, in spite of her threats, for we didn't blame her, we blamed him—this elusive stranger who sounded most frightfully strict, even stricter than Mother.

So we had a few more months to prepare in earnest for the homecoming of the "head of the family," and Mother was determined to be proud of her children, not ashamed, she explained with an anxious little frown. We promised to do our best to behave like perfect little angels and not to shock Father in any way.

"Now we will start with *food*," said Mother firmly. "You, Sarah, are the worst offender." I hung my head in shame.

"When I have a b-b-bad s-stomachache, I c-c-c-can't—" I began to excuse myself.

But Mother cut me short.

"When you have a bad stomachache, you are excused, and you have bread and milk. But you don't have a stomachache every day—do you, Sarah?"

"No," I mumbled, for I knew now what she had in mind.

"Very well. From today, you will have your *tapioca for tea* that you leave on your dinner plate."

I shuddered at the horrible suggestion. "Oh, Mother! Not all those b-b-beastly lumps?"

"Exactly."

We always had this beastly tapioca once a week, and I prayed with all my might that I should get a really bad stomachache that day; but, as usual, my prayers went unanswered, and I began to doubt the existence of this loving and merciful God we heard so much about.

Automatically I swallowed the smooth bits of tapioca and arranged the lumps around the edge of my plate.

"Have you forgotten already, Sarah? I mean what I say, you should know that," said Mother. "Well, don't say I didn't warn you."

No, I hadn't forgotten, but I was still hoping she would forget by teatime.

When I sat down to tea, she quietly opened the oven door and set the plate before me. I shuddered again, for the tapioca lumps looked even bigger and more revolting than they had earlier in the day.

William, just about to take a large bite of dripping toast (the butcher had a rota, and it was our turn for the dripping), stopped short and gave me a pitying glance.

Mary, always so tenderhearted, began to cry, and Henry, looking at the tapioca with eager anticipation, wondered what all the fuss was about.

"I c-c-can't," I wailed miserably. "It m-m-makes me feel s-s-sick."

William put his toast back on his plate and glared angrily across the table.

"Well, if she is sick, it will be all your fault!" he told Mother accusingly.

Mother retorted, "William! How *dare* you speak to your mother that way? When your father comes home—"

Her threat hung unfinished in mid-air, for I had

started on the tapioca. Four pairs of eyes watched in fascinated silence while I gulped and swallowed three of the largest lumps.

Mother's stern face relaxed, and she leaned across the table and scooped half of the remaining lumps onto her own plate and said with comforting reassurance, "Three! That's splendid, Sarah. Only three more mouthfuls and it's finished! Come, I'll race you!"

Still gulping and shuddering, I watched Mother swallow her share of the lumps as easily as she swallowed her tea.

Her eyes were kind now, and her manner part playful, part coaxing. She was, I am sure, in her own peculiar way as unhappy as her daughter at this additional threat to our pleasant teatime—for tea was our favorite meal, and a happy family reunion, at the end of the day.

Still the others waited, for William had given young Henry a stern look when he put his food to his mouth.

As the last lump slid down my throat, my plate was snatched away, and another appeared in the twinkling of an eye with a slice of hot dripping toast.

William grinned, Mary dried her eyes on her pinafore, and Henry demanded, "Can I start?" And I smiled at them, and loved them more than ever—especially Mother.

"Next week, I shall eat it for dinner," I promised.

Mother looked tremendously relieved. "That's a good girl, Sarah. You see, I don't want your father to think I have been spoiling you."

"Spoiling us? Gosh!" scoffed William, helping himself to another slice of hot dripping toast.

Mother ignored this remark and considered other ways we might improve ourselves before Father came home.

"But we are all right," grumbled William. "Do we have to be all that good to please Father, then? Why do we have to have a father, anyway?"

"William!" cried Mother in shocked disapproval. "You must never say such a dreadful thing again, especially in front of the little ones. Your father has been away too long, that's the trouble, and boys need a father," she added unconvincingly.

"*I* don't need a father, thank you!" argued William. "Anyway, I can't even remember what he looks like!" And he laughed carelessly.

"But you must remember your father," Mother implored. "You remember your father, don't you, Sarah?"

"Only a little teeny bit," I confessed sadly, for I could see she was really worried.

So she began to remind us of Father's curly red hair, his twinkling blue eyes, his bristling mustache, and his gaiety. He was strict, but also very gay, she insisted, and we should all have great fun. There would be presents for everyone and treats and parties galore, because Father was also very generous and kind. He liked to spend money, not save it. Indeed, you had only to mention something you wanted, and Father went out to buy it! We listened politely, but we didn't believe a word.

It was too late now to turn Father into a sort of benevolent Santa Claus. We knew better. Father was a strict disciplinarian who insisted on good manners and impeccable behavior. Father was a Regimental Sergeant Major who had to be obeyed, instantly.

"Don't want Father." Henry scowled at the military figure in the little frame.

Mother sighed as she gathered him onto her lap and explained, "Father will buy you a big horse on wheels you can push around the yard. You'll like that, Henry, won't you?"

"Don't want horse. Don't want Father," Henry repeated stubbornly.

Poor Mother! Poor Father!

Only Mary, it seemed, could be relied upon to behave nicely, for Mary might be shy of the strange father, but not willfully naughty, disobedient, or stubborn, for Mary was none of these things. (But I must remember to remind Father that you had to be gentle with Mary.)

We began to dread his homecoming, but could talk of nothing else.

Yet still the weeks went by and he didn't come. Why? Perhaps he was lost in the desert?

"Perhaps the ship has sunk to the bottom of the sea," William suggested to me in a hoarse whisper, and he added defiantly, "Serves him right, anyway! We don't want him here!"

"C-c-can we b-b-belong to chapel and not church? please, Mother," I begged one Sunday morning shortly before Easter.

"Certainly not!" she replied automatically. Then, a little curious, "Why?"

"B-b-because they have s-s-simply lovely Good Fridays!" I told her excitedly, "With t-t-tea-parties and c-c-concerts and everybody in their new Easter clothes! P-p-please let us join the chapel, Mother. They have t-t-treats in the winter and t-t-treats in the summer and lovely b-b-books for prizes."

Mother looked a little puzzled by this outburst. "I do wish you would try to talk slowly, Sarah, then you wouldn't stutter so badly. Tea parties and Easter clothes on Good Friday? Are you sure?"

I nodded vigorously.

"How very odd, but Good Friday is a sacred day," she mused thoughtfully. Though it must be confessed she found the three-hour service in church just a little tedious. And apart from hot cross buns and a picnic in the woods, we children hardly recognized Good Friday as a sacred day.

"What do you think about joining the chapel, William?" Mother inquired of her first-born when he sauntered down to breakfast.

"They have jolly good treats," he answered promptly, helping himself to Grape-nuts.

"Treats? Is that the only reason why so many children go to chapel Sunday School?"

William nodded.

"Very well, you may go to chapel," Mother decided after giving the matter much careful consideration. "But what shall I tell the Vicar when he calls?"

Good Friday, as usual, dawned bright and sunny, and we started to prepare for our first outing of the year soon after breakfast.

We had a three-mile walk to our favorite woods, and we set out, with Henry in a pushcart (Mary would take a turn for a ride when she tired), a flask of tea, sandwiches, cake, and apples. We hurried along the highway at a brisk pace until we reached the signpost pointing to the woods—almost a forest, for it stretched for several miles.

The narrow lane soon became nothing more than a cart track as we climbed over a stile.

In the deep muddy ditches, I found small clusters of primroses and celandines, and dragged Mary down to pick them. We were as pleased and excited as though we had found the pot of gold at the end of the rainbow.

William searched the hedges for birds' nests, and Henry climbed out of his pushcart to walk in the ditch, caring neither for flowers nor birds.

"Doesn't it smell nice?" breathed Mother ecstatically, sitting patiently on a stile.

We stopped at the gamekeeper's cottage on the edge of the wood for William to fill a large bottle with icy-cold water from the well.

The gamekeeper's wife ran out to exclaim excitedly, "Why, it's you again! It do seem a long time since last September, don't it now? My, but the baby's growed a fine big boy. But they be all fine bonny children, that I will say, and do you great credit. I mind the first time you came this way, with only the two, just toddling, as it were, and pretty as a picture in that there pushcart." Mother glowed with pride, while we stood around impatiently, waiting to be off to the woods.

"Gosh! She talks too much," William complained when at last we could get away from the garrulous old woman.

"Don't be unkind. The poor soul sees nobody all the winter, apart from her husband and her dog," Mother reminded him.

"Why does she stay there, then?" asked William with complete indifference. Then, not wanting an answer, he ran on ahead and disappeared into the forest of tall bracken.

I soon gave chase, dragging Mary behind me and dropping most of the precious wild flowers we had gathered so carefully. Mother picked them up as we ran, and called out, "Don't get lost now. See if you can find our picnic tree."

It was a giant oak tree, with spreading roots, and I knew exactly where to find it, though we hadn't seen it since last September. There was no sign of William, but he had taken a long draft of water and left the bottle propped against the tree.

Mother sat down with a great sigh of relief and contentment to have a cup of tea, while we children drank the water.

Then she closed her eyes for a moment and took a deep breath.

"It's a mixture of pine and fern and earth," she told us quietly, remembering her childhood on the farm in Surrey.

"Do you remember, Sarah, when we came here last September?"

I nodded, for I did remember.

She smiled. "You see, you have remembered. You thought you had forgotten all this in the winter when you were so miserably cold. But it's always there, tucked away in the back of your mind. This is something precious—something you will never forget. That is why we are here. That is why we tramp three long miles to get here, and three miles back. I want you to remember it, Sarah, all your life. Now go and play."

Henry was marching solemnly around and around the tree, waving a stick and driving an imaginary horse. William would only come back when he was hungry.

"Let's play mothers and fathers and make a little house," I suggested to Mary.

But when she obediently lay down to sleep, I was surprised and disappointed, for the game had only just started.

So I sat in the little house of ferns, hugging my knees, and wondered whether the fairies danced in the wood at night.

I wondered what it would be like to live always in the wood, and never go home. Supposing I changed into a rabbit and lived in a nest—no, burrow? Or a little red squirrel, with a frisky tail? I would rather be a squirrel.

I wondered who curled the edges of the ferns and who changed them from this cool delicious green to golden brown in September.

Supposing I had wings and could fly like that bird —where should I fly? I wish I had wings!

"Mary! It's time to wake up," I reminded my quiet little sister somewhat impatiently.

Then, because she looked so dazed and frightened in a wilderness of bracken, I gave her a hug and rushed her quickly back to Mother.

We had finished our share of the sandwiches and were already starting on the cakes when William sauntered through the trees, grinning amiably.

"Now look here, my lord, next time you are late, you will find nothing but an empty bag!" warned Mother without malice. (She often called William "my lord" now, because he was getting to be very arrogant.)

William lay flat on his stomach and reached for a sandwich.

"Gosh! I like it here" was all he said, but it was echoed in all our hearts.

Good Friday at chapel was all it was supposed to be, and more.

Dressed in our new Easter clothes (provided by the "Aunties" in Worthing), we all set out shortly before three-thirty P.M., after our long walk back from the woods. The tea party was an open invitation to children and parents alike, so Mother and Henry came, too. We joined the long queue at the schoolroom door, and Mother, with some misgiving, asked several other mothers whether we were trespassing on their hospitality, since we had never till this moment entered the chapel precincts. On being assured that all were welcome, Mother led her small brood rather shyly to one of the crowded trestle tables.

"Gosh!" exclaimed William. "*Two* kinds of bread and butter, *two* kinds of jam, *two* kinds of cake, *and* hot cross buns!"

"Hush," whispered Mother, blushing with embarrassment, as she tied on Henry's bib.

"Are you chapel now?" we were asked. And we had only to nod agreement over mugs of steaming hot tea, and we were accepted. It was as simple as that.

"Goodness gracious me!" Mother exclaimed after a hearty tea and an even heartier cantata in the chapel. "Have I been mistaken all these years? I always understood that Good Friday was a *sacred* day?"

"Both sacred and joyous, my dear sister!" boomed a faithful follower of Charles Wesley. "We should rejoice in our salvation, should we not?"

Mother looked doubtful. It was certainly a new conception, and worthy of consideration.

"Perhaps you are right," she said as she gathered us together on the steps of the chapel, ready to shake hands with a great many people and to say, "Thank you for having me."

"A pleasure! Delighted! Come again!" they called after us.

So, from that day, we "belonged" to chapel!

4
Father Takes a Bow

The telegram was delivered one Sunday morning. Mother flushed a rosy pink as she tore it open, and her hands trembled so violently we looked at her in dismay.

"Arriving Monday by twelve-thirty train. Love to all. Edward."

In spite of the long years of waiting and so many warnings, we all seemed paralyzed by shock, and stood there staring fixedly at the flimsy piece of paper in open-mouthed astonishment.

Till Mother, with a sudden wail of realization, exclaimed, "Monday? But that's *tomorrow*—and it's washing day!"

And that was the start, for nothing was ever the same again, till father went away—forever.

For the first time in our young lives, we saw Mother

disturbed and flustered, and her hands trembled all that day. Her face, still unnaturally flushed, had the same expression of doubt and helplessness as young Henry had when stricken by a sudden attack of biliousness.

After she had collapsed onto a chair, she asked rather pathetically, "Could someone make me a cup of tea?"

We all rushed to put on the kettle, find the teapot, the tea caddy, sugar, and milk. Mary brought one of the Sunday cups and saucers from the front-room china cabinet, and Henry found a teaspoon.

Poor Mother! What had gone wrong? Shouldn't we be excited and happy?

Mother watched us gravely, and when at last William presented her with a cup of very weak tea, sickly sweet—we forgot she had not taken sugar in her tea since the early days of the war—she was so touchingly grateful we felt we had achieved a major operation.

"Thank you, children." Her smile was warm and tender.

She drank every drop with apparent relish, while we stood around her waiting for her leadership.

William picked up the telegram and read it aloud, just in case there should be some mistake. But there was no mistake. *Father was coming home!* That legendary figure in the silver frame was actually real.

It was all too much for Mary, and she began to cry, softly and silently, her little face puckered in bewilderment.

"But why is Mary crying?" asked Mother in a small puzzled voice.

"And why am I sitting here?" She gave herself a shake. "Your father's coming home! Isn't it wonderful?

77

Tomorrow you will take a holiday from school, and I shall take a holiday from the washtub! We shall all dress up in our Sunday best clothes and go to the station to meet him! What will he say, I wonder, when he sees his children again—after four long years? Mary was the baby when he went away. Why, he hasn't even seen Henry!"

"Why hasn't Father seen Henry?" William demanded.

"Because he wasn't yet born."

"Why wasn't he born?"

"That will do, William—no more questions now, there's a good boy."

William frowned thoughtfully. "I remember, you sent us away to stay with Mrs. Summerfield, and when we came back Henry was there."

"That's right," Mother agreed. She was desperately anxious to change the subject, for she herself found it rather indelicate, and she still blushed when she thought of those four days with Edward on embarkation leave—in that dreadful hotel . . .

"Now, you will remember all I've told you, won't you? I want to be proud of you, and I want Father to be proud of you—not ashamed. You see, he will expect certain high standards of behavior, and he will expect you to obey instantly, you understand, because he is accustomed to giving orders, and having those orders instantly obeyed."

"M-m-my father is a Regimental Sergeant M-m-major," I repeated dutifully.

"Exactly," Mother agreed, with a worried little frown.

We all solemnly promised to be good, obedient, dutiful children, and Mother was satisfied.

It was now too late for Sunday School and too late for chapel and almost too late for dinner, so we had boiled eggs and cake.

"I want a proper dinner," grumbled Henry.

"Your father used to enjoy my apple pie, so we will keep it for tomorrow," Mother decided.

"Please, God, send a fine day tomorrow and make Mother happy again, and help me to obey Father. Amen."

I climbed into bed with Mary half an hour earlier than usual, "to get a good night's rest ready for the Great Day."

That was Mother's excuse, but I knew she really wanted extra time to catch up on the jobs she had to do, because it was one of her fixed rules, "Never put off till tomorrow what should be done today."

It was midsummer now, and our summer clothes, unlike our winter clothes, were mostly white or cream, and starched. Mary and I still wore starched pinafores, petticoats, and pants, and even our handkerchiefs were starched! William by this time had graduated to gray.

Mary fell asleep in my arms, but I lay awake for ages listening to the church clock chiming the quarter hours, till Mother came upstairs to bed at ten o'clock. Wondering and worrying about the morrow, I heard the hour of midnight strike and watched the moon sailing majestically across the starry sky.

What was Father really like?

Would he beat us if we disobeyed—like Emily's father?

Would he "swear like a trooper" and "drink like a fish"—like Ethel's father?

Would he insist that we leave chapel and go back to church?

Would he ask me a simple question that I couldn't answer? (He didn't know I stuttered.) Would he want to change simply everything—and would Mother allow him to change everything?

Father was coming home, and, although I searched my mind and memory till my head ached, I could remember only one thing about him.

Four years ago, he used to toss me in the air and catch me as I fell. I was terrified! Of course he could see I was much too big for that sort of game now.

But what if he did the same to Mary? He mustn't! I must warn him. She would probably die of fright, anyway. Henry wouldn't mind being tossed in the air, but not by a strange father. He was very much "Mother's boy" and shy of strangers.

As for William? I was even more worried about William's reactions to the strict parent who had to be obeyed instantly or else.

William obeyed when he was ready to obey, and often angered and annoyed Mother. Then, what new method could Father use on this intractable son? (If he beats him, I shall scream and bite! Yes, I shall hate Father if he hurts William.)

"Wake up, Sarah! It's seven o'clock."

"But it c-can't be. I've only been to s-sleep five minutes," I grumbled, and yawned.

Mother handed me a mug of tea.

"B-b-but it's M-M-Monday."

Then I saw our Sunday best clothes laid out on the chair, and our polished shoes in a neat row, and I looked at Mother and burst into tears.

•   •   •

Lined up in military precision on the quiet country station, we presented "as pretty a picture as I've see'd for many a long day." With this encouraging start from Mr. William Giles, the porter-cum-signalman-cum-opener of gates, we were content to wait for the train's arrival. Mother, looking tall and gracious in a sweeping skirt, white tailored blouse, white gloves, and black straw hat (freshly trimmed last night with a large and stiff bow of white ribbon), held the hands of Mary and Henry, while I linked up with Mary's other hand.

William stood stiffly to attention two yards to my left, his dark eyes glowing like two little lamps in his tense face. I recognized that look. William was ready for battle! Henry, in the white sailor suit, looked perfectly angelic.

For the first time, this Easter, the Aunties had presented us with identical frocks, that is, identical in pattern and design, but mine was smocked in blue, and Mary's in pink. The material was called tussore silk, and the deep hems allowed for growing. They would be our "best" frocks for two seasons, and then our "second-best," Mother had decided. We also wore identical straw hats wreathed in buttercups, spotless white gloves, socks, and shoes.

Mary's hair curled prettily around her tiny face, while mine hung in shining splendor almost to my waist.

"Are you proud of us, Mother?" I asked anxiously.

She smiled along the line. "Very proud!" she assured me. "Ah—here comes the train!"

Only one passenger stepped off the train, so it seemed that Father had chartered it especially for his own convenience. Five pairs of eyes stared fixedly at a door at the far end of the third coach as it swung open and a short sturdy figure, immaculate in khaki uniform, stepped out briskly. (I had imagined a giant, but he seemed much shorter than Mother.)

He was carrying a cane and neatly folded gloves in one hand, while he dragged onto the platform a large suitcase and a big black box plastered with labels. He signaled with his cane to the driver, and the train moved off slowly and jerkily.

Nobody had said a word.

Glancing nervously at Mother for leadership, I saw her face quivering nervously under the stiff white bow, and her eyes swimming with tears.

Then Father strode importantly down the platform, leaving his luggage behind, swept off his peaked cap ("Gosh! an officer's cap," muttered William, much impressed), and grinned boyishly. "Hello! Here we are at last!" he said.

The grin was William's grin, and the bright blue eyes were Henry's, but the flaming red hair shocked and surprised me. (Mother's hair was black, already tinged with gray, and we children had fair or brown hair.) The military mustache was so much more imposing in real life than in the photograph.

Wrapping Mother in a bear's hug, he kissed her eagerly and passionately on her smiling mouth, while Henry hid his face in her skirt and Mary looked up shyly at the red-haired stranger. We waited impatiently to be noticed, but for a long moment we were completely ignored and forgotten, while they smiled into each other's eyes and murmured soft endearments we could neither hear nor understand.

It was Mother who recovered first and, shaking herself free of those fierce encircling arms, turned shiny-eyed as a young girl to her little family. "Well, dear—what do you think of the children?" she asked tremulously.

Then his twinkling blue eyes swept along the line. "Marvelous! Splendid! I've never seen a better turned out family in my life! They do you great credit, my dear." And he kissed Mother again. Then he gave me a special smile of recognition. "Sarah darling, you haven't changed at all," he told me. And he squatted low on his heels, opened wide his arms, and, gathering Mary on one arm and me on the other, hugged and kissed us both so fiercely we were quite breathless.

"Daddy loves you very much, you know that, don't you? And it wasn't my fault that I had to stay away so long. Didn't Mummy explain to you?"

We nodded gravely and straightened our hats, still too shy to speak.

"Aren't they adorable? Aren't they pretty?" he demanded of Mother.

Then, putting us gently back on our feet, he tried to coax Henry out of Mother's skirt. But Henry remained hidden.

"He's very shy, but he will be all right later," Mother explained, with her arm encircling her youngest child protectively.

William had neither moved nor spoken, but stood stiffly erect watching his father gravely.

Till he felt his shoulders grasped in a grip of steel, and a pair of shrewd, searching eyes traveling over his trim little figure.

"Well, my son? Have you nothing to say?" asked Father.

William blushed and wriggled uncomfortably. For the first time in his life he was unsure of himself. Should he shake hands with this rather alarming person, or was he expected to kiss him?

But Father, it seemed, was only teasing, and his stern face relaxed while he gathered his eldest son to his heart. Meeting Mother's lingering glance over the top of William's dark head, he smiled tenderly and lovingly.

"I can't believe it. I must be dreaming. Tell me I'm not dreaming," he implored her—as I would say myself to Mother after waking from a nightmare.

She smiled back at him reassuringly. "No, you are not dreaming."

Then he sighed a great tearing sigh and, holding William at arm's length, again inquired, but gently, pleadingly, "Nothing to say, my son?"

"Welcome home, Father," said William promptly, for he had forgotten his long-rehearsed speech.

"Thank you, William."

"Well, shall we go home? Have you ordered a taxi, my dear?"

"Taxi?" Mother repeated in a puzzled sort of way, for we walked everywhere—and we all had walked the mile to the station, including Henry. "I believe old Herbert Hodge still runs a taxi in the village, but I didn't think—I mean—I'm sorry."

"Quite all right, my dear—don't let it worry you," said Father soothingly. Cupping his hands to his mouth, he yelled across the station, "Hi! You there! Bill Giles! Come on out and show yourself, you old son of a gun!"

And the startled face of the porter peered around the door. "Morning, sir—welcome home," he stammered.

"Good morning to you," said Father briskly. "Just phone up Herbert Hodge, there's a good fellow, and ask him to come along to the station right away. Then you might give me a hand with that box over there."

"Yes, sir. Certainly, sir."

"My sainted aunt!" muttered Father. "Does he always move at that pace?"

"With only three trains a day, why should he hurry?" Mother suggested in her calm, quiet way.

And Father threw back his head and laughed. It was a loud rip-roaring shout of laughter that echoed through the deserted station and across the fields of golden corn shimmering in the hot midday sun. It was laughter such as we had never heard before—gay, infectious, and wholly masculine.

William's grave little face suddenly crumpled, then he, too, was laughing madly and smacking his thighs. They looked so comic, I started to giggle, then I felt this same wild laughter spilling out of me, while Father's big strong hands spun me around and around like a top.

Mother caught my flying hat as it bounced along the platform.

"Goodness gracious me!" she exclaimed, looking at her long-lost husband with some misgiving. Was he always so noisy and boisterous? she wondered a little anxiously.

"The taxi! The taxi!" screamed William, streaking down the platform to be first to climb in.

The old cab shuddered to a halt, and a dirty wrinkled face put his head out to say plaintively, "She don't seem too sure of 'erself today, guvnor. Likely as not she'll stop altogether 'alfway up that there 'ill."

Father, ready to explode again, was quickly hushed

by Mother, and we all climbed in to join William. The porter was dragging the heavy box and suitcase onto his truck, while Father, with cane tucked under his arm and peaked cap at a jaunty angle over his bushy eyebrows, directed operations.

The driver groaned as the heavy box clattered in beside him, and pulled on his whiskers.

"I don't think she'll take it, guvnor."

"Of course she'll take it!" Father grinned at the two old men, gave them each a coin, and climbed into the cab.

"My sainted aunt! Call this a taxi? I should think he dug it out of the British Museum!" he exclaimed.

"Edward, please," pleaded Mother as she gathered Henry onto her lap.

Mary was scooped onto Father's knee, where she sat, smiling shyly at this bold and boisterous stranger.

Squeezed between Father and Mother, I hoped that everyone would see us.

Mother waved a gloved hand like a queen as we purred and panted up the village street in a cloud of steam.

"Why all the steam?" yelled Father.

The driver shrugged.

"She always lets off a dratted lot of steam, guvnor, but it don't mean a thing—like my old woman!" he chortled.

Father was delighted at our reception and waved his cap from the other window.

"Everybody knows you are c-c-coming home to-day," I told him importantly.

"Thank you, darling." He kissed the tip of my nose.

"Look! Even the Vicar is waving to us!" William

exclaimed, so Father leaned out, saluted smartly, and called "Good morning, sir!" as we rattled past.

Father was wonderful! I liked him. I hoped he would like me.

The first meal with Father at the head of the table was hurried, because we were anxious to get the box unpacked.

The box had very strong padlocks and had traveled thousands of miles with Father. I half expected to see a genie emerge, for it looked to me like a magic box. In a way, it *was* magic, for it was full of presents and curious things from Mesopotamia. We three were crowded around it on the floor, but Henry, still clinging to Mother, climbed on her lap for protection.

On top of the box, wrapped in soft tissue paper, was a beautiful stole, in ivory satin, embroidered in exotic patterns, with vivid splashes of red, purple, and gold. Father draped it lovingly around Mother's shoulders, and she kissed him.

"Stand up and turn about," he told her. And she stood up obediently and turned about while we all admired her.

"It's for evening wear—dinner parties and such like," said Father vaguely as he reached for more packages. Father didn't understand, of course, but Mother never went out in the evening; she always stayed at home. But it was a lovely present.

Mary had a pretty doll dressed in a sari, and Henry a toy train, and William received a penknife with an ivory handle.

"Gosh, thanks!" He was very pleased with it and started to sharpen all our pencils.

My present was a dear little needlework box, with

cotton, scissors, and thimble, because Mother had mentioned in one of her weekly letters to Father that I could now sew quite nicely.

And we all started hugging and kissing all over again. Henry was obliged to say "thank you" but stubbornly refused to do more than that. I could see that Father was a little disappointed, for when he opened his arms and tried to coax his youngest child with soft endearments, Henry turned his face away. He was unaccustomed to baby talk and probably jealous of this red-haired man kissing his beloved mother.

Several yards of Indian silk, to be made into summer frocks "for the girls," pleased Mother enormously. Then came two pairs of heavy curtains richly embroidered in wool. But our windows were small, with lattice panes.

"I shall hang them on the doors," said Mother quickly, before I could voice some stupid remark.

Under the curtains lay a most extraordinary collection of things that Father had bought in an Eastern market. We all helped to take them out of the box and arrange them on the table, while Mother, her beautiful stole draped over her apron, wondered where on earth she was going to put everything.

There were tall vases and short vases, vases with dragons, and vases with queer Hindustani inscriptions, boxes for jewelry (though Mother had only two brooches), ashtrays galore, a number of carved sandalwood elephants, and one large white marble elephant ("Elephants are lucky, did you know?" said Father). And a collection of daggers—at which Mother screamed, "Edward, please put those horrid knives away!"

There were jugs and jars, plates and pots—all fashioned by natives in the bazaars—and a model of the famous tomb, the Taj Mahal, in small marble sections, to be built up like a jigsaw puzzle that same evening.

Mother was trying hard to appreciate all these wonderful treasures from Mesopotamia, but I could see she was glancing anxiously around her crowded little front room and trying to place them, in her mind.

The Taj Mahal would have a place of honor, under a glass case, Father decided, and he himself would build and erect a corner cabinet with several useful shelves to display the rest.

Had Mother forgotten what a handy man he was with a hammer and chisel? "We must move out one of the armchairs, then, and possibly that little occasional table," said Mother doubtfully, for she was rather fond of "occasional" tables draped in starched white cloths.

"They will have to be dusted very carefully, Sarah," Mother reminded me, for I had recently been promoted to dusting (as well as brass doorknobs and drying up the dishes). This extra duty would mean less time for reading my favorite books and for writing my stories and verses. But Father was a wonderful person, and I decided to overlook his passion for exotic possessions.

Henry was being promoted from a cot in Mother's room to a camp bed in William's room, but it was not until bedtime that he realized the full implication of such a move. When he did, he roared, "I want my cot!" Kicking and screaming, he was carried to the strange little bed, but his screams of rage brought Father leaping upstairs to assist Mother in the battle. She shook her head and pushed him away. She was still wearing the stole and the apron, and her face was flushed and troubled when she came downstairs some time later, because of Henry's naughtiness. "He's usually such a good little boy," she explained to Father. "But he's not to blame. It's my fault entirely. I should have moved him into William's room weeks ago, then he would have had time to get used to it."

Father made no comment, but he quietly picked up his suitcase and went upstairs to unpack.

After a few undecided moments, I took Mary's hand, and we followed him. We stood rather shyly in the doorway watching Father spread his clothes on Mother's bed—suits and shirts and ties and socks, slippers, dressing gown, pajamas, hairbrushes, and razor.

Fascinated by this unfamiliar sight, I said slowly and truthfully, "Mother has never had a m-m-man in her b-b-bedroom b-before."

Father looked up with twinkling eyes, opened wide his arms, and we rushed into them.

"My darlings—Daddy loves you very much."

We clung to him, hugging and kissing his sunburned cheeks, pulling on his mustache, rumpling his crisp curly hair.

I told him I wanted him to wear his uniform all the time, because then I could show him to everyone.

He grinned and promised to wear it for a week or so, but after that he would be discharged from the army and be very thankful to be a civilian again.

"Now, shall I put you to bed?" he asked. "It's getting late, isn't it?"

"We put ourselves to bed," Mary told him importantly, and he pretended to be very surprised at our cleverness and promised to come in to kiss us good night.

We crept in to look at Henry, and he had fallen

asleep outside the bedclothes. His face was flushed and wet with tears. Poor little Henry. He cried every night for a week or more and never forgave Father for turning him out of Mother's bedroom.

Every day now was a Special Day, with some fresh surprise or treat or promise of a treat in store for us. Father was determined to make up to us, he said, all the good things we had missed in four long years of war and separation.

Mother reminded him that food was still rationed and scarce, but he only laughed and told her to leave everything to him, for all her worries were over.

So Father took over the shopping and the cooking, and we lived like fighting cocks! He bribed the butcher, the baker, the publican, and the postman to provide us with juicy steaks, chickens, ducks, rabbits, and hares.

Everything was lavishly flavored with onions and garnished with mushrooms! I was sick every day but came up for more! Such an orgy of food and feasting! But Mother was anxious lest we get accustomed to extravagant living, and constantly reminded us it was only temporary—until Father settled down.

But Father showed no sign of ever "settling down" and continued to enjoy himself and to give his children "the time of their lives." He was noisy and boisterous, quick-tempered and affectionate—and I adored him! So did Mary. Such spoiling and petting, kissing and hugging, such lavish presents and such lovely parties. Our friends were green with envy, for none could boast a father like ours.

One morning at breakfast, he served us all with

generous portions of bacon and mushrooms, looked at each of us in turn, and grinned.

We knew he had thought of something nice. "Now, I want each one of you to think hard and then ask me for something *special*," he began. "By that I mean something you have been wanting very badly for a long time, and your Mother either couldn't afford to buy it or it couldn't be found in the local shops. Well, now is your chance, for whatever you choose, I shall get for you, by hook or by crook. I promise you that."

Mother looked uncomfortable.

"Really, dear, you are spoiling them dreadfully," she sighed. "They really have all they need."

I was sorry to contradict her, but I hadn't. "C-c-could I have a d-doll, a p-p-proper d-d-doll?" I pleaded.

"But Sarah, you are getting too big for a doll." Mother objected.

But Father was on my side.

"If Sarah wants a doll, she shall have a doll." And he gave me an encouraging wink. "And you, William?"

"I want a gun," said William promptly, glancing slyly at Mother, who had flatly refused to have any kind of weapon in the house. William even had to hide his catapult.

"A gun? Do you mean a revolver or a rifle?" asked Father, not in the least surprised by his son's request for firearms.

"A rifle—and a lot of cartridges," William added decisively.

Father agreed and turned to Mary.

" I don't know." Mary was perfectly content with her few toys and her dolls, and seemed surprised to be asked such a funny question.

"Perhaps a doll's tea set, then? She's always having tea parties," Mother suggested.

And Mary smiled and said that would do.

"And what would Henry like?"

Henry closed his mouth over his bacon and stared blankly at his plate. He just wouldn't talk to Father at all, unless he was absolutely obliged, and I thought Father was getting a little annoyed and frustrated by Henry's stubbornness. "Never mind, don't bother. I'll get him a wooden horse on wheels," he told Mother when she tried to insist on a polite answer.

"And Mother shall have a brand-new bicycle—we both will have bicycles, my dear, and ride around the country lanes in style! I hate walking, anyway!" And with that parting shot, Father went off to Tunbridge Wells—by taxi.

We used the front room every day now and not only on Sundays, and the presents were laid out for our inspection when we came home from school. The bicycles, costing the fabulous sum of seven guineas each, were being delivered later.

The doll, for which I had longed so passionately when I was seven, was a little late to receive the affection she deserved, but I liked her well enough for another two years or so.

"I had to visit every toy shop in town to find her, darling," Father explained as I lifted her gently out of the long box. "You see, all the best dolls come from Germany, and we haven't imported any during the war, and still can't buy a German doll for love or money. I'm sorry, but I'm afraid she has a false wig, and her eyes don't close, and her legs won't bend. Apparently she has to spend her days standing up, and go to sleep with her eyes open!"

"It doesn't m-m-matter, she's b-beautiful," I assured him, and smothered him with grateful hugs and kisses.

William, in the meantime, had raced upstairs with his air gun, to practice shooting from a bedroom window, followed by Mother, urging him to be careful and not to shoot any birds.

"Haven't we had enough of war and guns?" She spoke rather sharply to Father, because of her new anxiety.

"My dear, it's as natural for a boy to want a gun as a girl to want a doll," said Father complacently as he laid out Mary's tea set on the table and pushed the wooden horse into Henry's reluctant hands.

The bicycles were delivered the following day, so Mother was obliged to leave her chores, put on her hat and gloves, and prepare for her first lesson. Father had anticipated a short period of demonstration, whereupon Mother would mount her saddle, and fly away easily and joyfully. But his hopes were dashed to the ground, for not only had Mother no balance at all, but no sense of direction. Day after day, they followed the same procedure in the quiet country lane (we sometimes followed them and hid in the hedge).

"Watch me, my dear," Father would say as he pedaled furiously down the lane, made a neat detour, and returned, waving his hand to prove how simple it all was.

"Now, you try—don't be nervous—and bend your back a little, dear. There, that's fine, just relax. It's so easy."

Mother, in hat and gloves, and dignified silence, clutched the handlebars as a drowning man clutches a lifebelt, started slowly on her perilous journey.

"I've got you! You're doing fine!" yelled Father, supporting her from behind and trotting briskly alongside.

But the instant he removed his hand, Mother gave a frightened little shriek, steered straight for the hedge, and tumbled off in the brambles!

With her usual persistence, however, she persevered. "If at first you don't succeed, *try again!*" William was quick to remind her, so she couldn't give up!

At last, after many weeks of practice, they both appeared riding side by side on the high road, and we held our breath as a wagon rumbled past, and cheered when the accident was averted. They both had won a battle in a way, I suppose, for Father was determined that Mother should learn to ride the new bicycle, and "enjoy" the pleasures of cycling to other villages. But Mother's "enjoyment" was so alien to Father's, and not to be found on the highway!

Gradually she excused herself, and Father went off alone—to explore . . .

All that lovely summer our friends were invited to parties and picnics, and we tasted such luxuries as strawberries and cream, iced cakes, and fizzy lemonade for the first time. The boys still preferred Mother's homemade lemonade, and she made it fresh for them each day with lemons and brown sugar in a bedroom jug wreathed in roses.

After a few months, the pattern of our lives had so completely changed I could hardly recall the time, not so long ago, when Father was just a figure in a silver frame.

His loud rip-roaring laughter no longer surprised or startled me, but I was still afraid of his sudden anger, his flashing eyes, and stern voice—and so was Mary.

But not William. William was bold and brave as ever.

A gradual change crept into our family with the passing of summer, picnics and parties, treats and outings, and the novelty of having such a generous father.

Now an almost constant battle was waged between father and son—a battle of wills that Mother watched with ever increasing fear and anxiety, for both her husband and her son had violent, uncontrollable tempers.

I had a rather objectionable habit of listening on the stairs, and once I heard Mother say in a calm, cold voice, "Punish him, then, in any way you want, but don't thrash the boy. In anger, you could do him a grievous injury. You are terribly strong, Edward, and the boy is nothing more than a child. If you do thrash him, I shall never forgive you." I shivered at the icy calm of her voice and ran back upstairs—to finish the dusting!

And now I was torn apart, and my loyalty divided. Mother was right. She was always right. I should hate Father if he beat William.

But I didn't want to hate Father, and I was desperately anxious we all should be happy together, all the time.

But William was being deliberately defiant and difficult, and young Henry had not accepted his father, so they practically ignored each other now.

One Saturday in late autumn, William strolled in to dinner when we had almost finished, and met the fury of his father's smoldering eyes quite calmly.

"Where have you been?" Father demanded. "And what have you been doing since nine o'clock?"

William shrugged. "Nothing—just mooching around."

Father's eyes blazed, and his eyebrows twitched with annoyance.

"When I ask a civil question, William, I expect a civil answer."

William looked surprised. Mother had always seemed completely satisfied with that answer, hadn't she?

Father's fist crashing on the table upset the water, and upset Mary. She began to cry.

"Don't be c-c-cross with William!" I wailed.

"My sainted aunt!" groaned Father, covering his face with his hands. "What a family!"

"Go to your room, William," said Mother, quietly —and he went without another word.

But patience was not a quality that Father would ever possess, and he grew more and more impatient, not only with his children but with the aftermath of war. Suddenly he was forced to realize he must find a job, for he had spent lavishly, and now his money was dwindling.

But what had a small remote Kentish village to offer a man of such intelligence and ability? Where could this restless, rebellious redhead find the interesting and absorbing occupation his talents demanded? He spoke fluent Arabic and was a born leader of men, and his soul craved for fresh fields to conquer.

Already torn between love and loyalty to his family and the stronger compelling urge to be free, he became more and more irritable, moody, and depressed. He began to think of going back to Baghdad.

But he didn't tell Mother, yet . . .

One day I found him nursing Mary on his knees, with Mother and William standing over him. She was sobbing in that completely heartbroken way we had not heard for some time.

"But why do you speak so sharply, when you know how sensitive she is?" Mother scolded, and William added, "You have to be gentle with Mary."

Father's face crumpled helplessly.

"I'm sorry, darling, truly sorry," he pleaded. Poor Father! Poor Mother! How would it all end?

I was desperately anxious that Father should love me—too anxious.

He was at first amused, then embarrassed, and finally irritated by my constant fussing. He didn't want a hassock to his feet or a cushion to his head! I began to walk in my sleep, and he was shocked and dismayed by this further peculiarity in his eldest daughter.

Once again, sitting on the stairs, I overheard them talking about me.

"Listeners never hear any good of themselves," Mother had warned me—and she was right.

"What seems to be the trouble with Sarah?" Father demanded.

"There is nothing the matter with Sarah," I heard Mother reply in that new "defensive" sort of voice.

"Nothing? You call stuttering and sleepwalking nothing? The child's a nervous wreck," Father insisted. "She needs to see a child's specialist. I'll take her to London. I'll—"

But Mother cut him short.

"You will not take Sarah to London. Surely you must allow me to know what is best for the child. After all, I've managed alone for four years. The child's just —well—*imaginative*, she will grow out of it."

"Well, I hope you are right, but she seems a queer

little soul at the moment, and, quite candidly, I don't understand her."

"But that's what you said about William," Mother pointed out gently. "Be patient, dear. Children must take their own time to develop in their separate individual ways."

And before I fled back upstairs, I heard him say quite clearly and distinctly, *"My darling girl."*

Was Mother his darling girl, then?

But Mother gradually became very silent and withdrawn, sitting for long moments gazing into the fire, her busy hands lying idle in her lap. Now her eyes were ringed with dark shadows.

Father would be moody, restless, and irritable for days on end, then suddenly playful and full of pranks as a young boy, so that we were no longer certain of anything—only that something was wrong. A brooding uneasiness spoiled the happy spontaneous moments we spent together as a family, and sometimes I would hear our parents deep in earnest conversation that ceased abruptly when the children arrived.

Then, as the wintry winds began to blow across the empty fields and whistle mournfully down the chimney, Father began to pack.

Once more we stood in the doorway, once more his clothes were laid out—clean, well-pressed civilian clothes.

Clutching Mary's hand, I asked him, "Where are you g-g-going, Father?" although I knew already he was going away.

"Come here to me, Sarah and Mary." He spoke very

quietly, and his face was sad and grave, the blue eyes troubled.

We went to him then and sat on his knees, and I looked at the clothes on the bed and the battered leather suitcase with its many labels, and burst into wild weeping, imploring him to stay. But my tongue was tied, and I could only make a strange jumble of sounds between my sobs because of this awful calamity that was happening to us again as a family, and because I was too young and too innocent to understand.

Mother was still the most wonderful mother in the world—but I wanted a father, too.

All my friends had envied me for a few short months, but they wouldn't envy me now.

So I sobbed despairingly on that strong shoulder, so soon to be removed. I had never realized before how very comforting a father's shoulder can be. Even my "stomachache" had been less uncomfortable, resting quietly on father's shoulder. Now I should have to "make do" with the sofa again and the big clumsy hot-water bottle. I sobbed afresh in an agony of self-pity.

Father held me close, murmuring tender endearments, until I could cry no more, then he began to explain carefully and gently why he had to leave us again.

He had accepted a very important post in Baghdad, and everything was going to be simply wonderful, if we would just be brave and patient for a few more months.

There would be a big new bungalow in Baghdad, with lots of native servants to do all the work, and when it was ready he would send for us.

"All of us?" I gulped. It had to be all of us, or I couldn't bear it.

"All of you," he agreed. "That's a solemn promise, darling. When everything is ready, I shall send for you, and we shall all be together again," he repeated.

"And live happy ever after?"

"And live happy ever after," he echoed.

So he dried our tears, and we smothered him with hugs and kisses and went downstairs to tell Mother.

He was still the most wonderful father in the whole world! Baghdad! What would my friends say now?

What an adventure!

With Father to welcome us like a king, and Mother to reign like a queen with all her native servants!

Mother was making toast for tea, and she asked without turning her head, "Have you told them?"

William was explaining to Henry that he couldn't borrow his pocketknife, but he could have a hammer instead.

"Why is your face so red?" she demanded.

"Sarah's been crying," Father explained quietly, still looking fixedly at the back of Mother's head.

Then I ran to her, threw my arms around her neck, and began to stammer out the exciting story father had told us, that he was going away, but soon we should all be together again in Baghdad!

That she hadn't to worry any more, for soon she would have servants to do all her work, like a real lady!

Still without turning her head, she told me, quite calmly, "We are not going to Baghdad, Sarah. Your father is going, but we are staying here."

Each word dropped slowly and separately, like pebbles in a pool.

Stunned and bewildered, I glanced imploringly from one to the other.

"Cheer up, darling! Mother will change her mind," said Father confidently.

I stared at him in blank astonishment. Surely he must know that Mother never changed her mind. Never!

Then she slowly turned her head to look at him, and her eyes shone so deep and dark in her flushed face, he was compelled to close his own eyes for a second to escape from their searching penetration. She seemed to be burning up inside with a passionate resentment more perplexing than anger.

But her voice had a chilling quality and a deadly calm.

"If you go back to Baghdad, you go alone," she told him. *"And the children stay here with me."*

Desperately I tried, again and again in the short time left to us, to persuade Father to stay or Mother to go.

It was like beating my head against a solid wall of adult opposition and obstinacy, for both were equally adamant, both were right, both had wills so strong and inflexible that I was bruised and battered, mentally and spiritually, before I gave up in despair one day, only to try fresh tactics the next.

I beseeched Father to take me, alone. I argued that Mother could manage quite nicely with William, Mary, and Henry. I couldn't bear it, I told him, that he had to go back alone to Baghdad, with nobody to love him— only those native servants.

"When you are a big girl, darling, you can be my housekeeper. There, that's a promise!" He held me close to his heart, and I had to be content with that.

• • •

Once more we went to the station, but now we were sad and silent in the rattling little cab, and nobody waved as we went through the village. There was nothing more to say, for everything had already been said so many times, and I had no more tears to cry.

But when the train whistled around the bend, I clutched his hand. Mary had the other, and she still could cry.

For the last time, we were gathered up together in those strong arms, kissed and hugged in a fierce embrace, and put gently back on our feet. William shook hands gravely, and Henry, for the last time, turned his head away.

Folding Mother in his arms, we heard Father say imploringly, for the last time, "You will change your mind, won't you? I shall have everything ready in six months."

Then he was gone—forever.

Exactly a year later, Mother was baking a cake one Saturday morning when another cablegram arrived. (Father was pelting her with letters and cables now, and William thought we should soon be on our way to Baghdad.)

"What does he say this time?" William demanded eagerly, and we all crowded around her.

Mother tore open the envelope with floured hands, read the contents, gave a little gasp, and sat down hurriedly on the kitchen table.

Slowly and distinctly she said, "Your father is dead."

5

Mother Takes a Lodger

Father's spirit came home to rest in me, his ten-year-old daughter, Sarah.

Father was not dead. It was inconceivable. He was the most alive person I had ever known. Besides, we had no funeral, no grave, no wreaths of carnations or crosses of lilies—so how could Father be dead?

Everybody had a funeral when they died. We watched from the window, peeping between drawn blinds, out of respect for the dead.

The gravedigger was a great friend of William's, for he spent all his spare time, when he was not digging graves, fishing in the river or studying bird life. William had an insatiable curiosity for both the fish and the birds. The river attracted him like a magnet, and Mother had tried to persuade him to promise not to go near the river until he had learned to swim. But he wouldn't be persuaded, and he didn't promise.

William, like Father, was a law unto himself. Neither the chains of love nor the chains of duty could bind them. I could see now, more clearly than ever before, that sturdy, self-confident figure stepping briskly off the train into our lives.

His every gesture was fresh in my memory—the cane tucked under his arm, the neatly folded kid gloves, the immaculate precision of his uniform dress, the jaunty angle of his peaked cap, his waxed mustache, sunburned cheeks, and piercing blue eyes, his strutting walk that reminded me of Cocky in the back yard, the boyish grin melting his stern features, his flaming red hair, and, finally, that loud rip-roaring masculine laugh.

I remembered his strong hands, both gentle and forceful; his voice, both tender and tempestuous; his erratic behavior, both impeccable and irresponsible.

I remembered the comfort of his shoulder to cry on, the warm hugs, and the hungry kisses.

I remembered that lovely word "darling" he had first introduced, but when he went away, "darling" went with him.

If it were true that Father was dead, why was he so inexplicably alive in me? And why did I suddenly feel so restless and rebellious, so eager to spread my wings, so conscious of Mother's disapproval?

If the father I adored was dead, my heart would weep, but my heart refused to weep.

I had to be reminded constantly by other people that this lively, loveable person would never again come back into our lives. (William had explained to me that Father had died very suddenly in a Baghdad hospital of enteric fever.) When I smiled unconsciously at the robin or the little brown hens or the hot cocoa and the dripping toast, William would scowl and whisper, "Have you forgotten? Father is dead. Can't you even look sorry?" And then he would remind me to tidy my hair.

I believe he suddenly felt the full responsibility of manhood on his twelve-year-old shoulders, and that is why he seemed so grave and dictatorial.

I hated the black hair ribbons tied to my long plaits, and the black cotton gloves I had to wear, even to school. But when one of the Aunties arrived from Worthing "to make the children's mourning clothes," I was interested and rather glad to have something new to wear. She brought all her materials with her and borrowed a sewing machine from one of the neighbors, and after a "good cry" over "poor dear Edward," lined us up in the kitchen to be measured for our new clothes. William declined to have homemade clothes, so she compromised by making him a black armband, which he wore with great distinction for three months. He also had a black tie and two new gray shirts from a shop at Tunbridge Wells.

Mother went off to Tunbridge Wells with a kind neighbor the day after she received the cablegram, and came back wearing a complete new outfit of clothes—all black. She continued to wear them for six months. With her dark eyes and olive skin, she looked very distinguished, I thought. Apart from shoes and stockings, Mother had not bought any new clothes since before the war, so it was not surprising that we hardly recognized the tall, dignified figure who stepped so quietly out of the taxi in her widow's weeds.

Only half-mourning for the children, Mother had decided, because we were so young.

Henry, still very mystified by all the fuss, and weary of being called a "poor little lamb," allowed himself to be measured for two new buster suits—lavender gray for weekdays, and cream trimmed with gray for Sundays.

Then came the girls' turn, at last, and once again it was decided that Mary and I should have identical frocks with matching knickers. Since our clothes had always been made to measure at Grandmother Prior's house, it was fascinating to watch them actually taking shape under our noses, so to speak.

We hung about the front room for three days, waiting to be told they were ready to wear.

Our school frocks, of black and white check gingham, with yoke and cuffs of pale mauve, were made in a simple pinafore style. We had two each of these.

Our Sunday frocks were much prettier, and I fell in love with mine at once and could hardly wait for Sunday to show it off. In a fine linen the color of rich cream, embroidered in lazy-daisy stitch of mauve and purple silk, and with wide matching belts, the Sunday frocks were much admired.

We had been sent home from school by the Headmaster, who had made a short but profoundly moving speech to the whole school about Father and his gallant exploits in Mesopotamia.

We were surprised to hear that he had "blown up an armored truck almost single-handed, routed a tribe of savage Turks, and escaped with his life on several occasions." We sang "Onward Christian Soldiers" and "Fight the Good Fight." We were kissed and hugged and cried over and finally sent home, far more upset by this mass demonstration than ever we had been by the cablegram or Mother's widow's weeds.

We hung around the kitchen all that day, restless and tearful, till bedtime, when Mother brought us mugs of steaming hot cocoa and kissed us good night with a great sigh of relief.

The next day we went back to school. Still Mother did not weep—or if she wept, she wept in secret, in the privacy of her bedroom, for Mother never again shared her bedroom with anyone.

A few weeks later, young Henry was promoted to the box room, in his camp bed, so that William, who was now "the man of the family," could have his own room at last.

It seemed that Mother was determined to carry on as though this shattering blow had never happened.

The neighbors, quick to offer sympathy and assistance, were met by this grave, tearless woman who politely refused all offers of help.

"Thank you—you are very kind, but I can manage," she told them.

Now the photograph in the silver frame had been removed from the kitchen mantelpiece to a place of honor on her bedside table. And she urged me to be specially careful with the Taj Mahal under its glass dome, because Father had thought very highly of it.

The big chunky corner shelves, which he had eventually bought at an auction sale because he was not clever with hammer and chisel, remained there throughout the rest of our childhood, with all Father's exotic collection of souvenirs laid out in splendid array. A heavy Persian rug gave an almost luxurious appearance now to the small front room—it was a present from Father to Mother on arrival in Baghdad, and probably intended to tempt Mother to change her mind. It provided me with a comfortable place on which to sprawl with a book on pleasant Sunday afternoons. After the rough coconut matting with which the floor had previously been covered, this lovely Persian rug with its rich colorings and vivid designs seemed to me the very essence of luxury. I even tried squatting cross-legged on it, wondering if it might turn out to be a magic carpet that would transport me to some far-distant Arabian market.

As I carefully dusted the little sandalwood camels and elephants and ran my fingers down the silk-embroidered dragons, I enjoyed delicious daydreams of these places with fascinating names—Bombay, Beirut, Baghdad, Calcutta, Cairo, Karachi.

Should I ever see them for myself? Should I ever be allowed to leave the village, to adventure and explore beyond the shores of England—beyond the horizon?

Should I meet Father wandering in an Eastern market?

I could feel inside me now not only an insatiable curiosity that was my heritage, but also this new awareness of other lands and other peoples.

It made me restless and furtive, and a little unhappy, because I felt it was wrong and disloyal to Mother.

Now I discovered I was torn apart, for I still loved Mother devotedly and thought she was the bravest and most wonderful mother in the world.

But I had adored Father, and longed passionately to see him again. In the few short months I had known a father, he had changed my ideas, my dreams, and my future. I was no longer content with fairy tales, *Mother Goose*, and the Bible.

I had to read *The Arabian Nights, Robinson Cru-*

soe, The Swiss Family Robinson, and even *Pilgrim's Progress!*

The Sunday School Superintendent was known as a "gentleman farmer"—and he lived in a mellowed manor house surrounded by fields and orchards with his two devoted sisters, Miss Kate and Miss Ruth. Together they managed to entertain and interest a swarm of children of all ages, from three to fourteen years, every Sunday morning for an hour—and every first Saturday in September. On this particular day, they entertained the entire Sunday School (plus mothers and babies) to the Summer Treat at Manor Farm.

Only once did the good Lord fail to answer the fervent prayer of the Superintendent for a fine day—and then we had to race for shelter in a heavy downpour to the great barn, where the indefatigable Miss Kate and Miss Ruth had laid tea on trestle tables amid the straw. Always we had two kinds of cake, plain and currant, from a baker at Tunbridge Wells, and an apple and orange to take away. While the rain beat relentlessly on the timbered roof, we sat inside, snug and warm and drowsy with the sweet smell of hay and apples in the hayloft.

Only once did we have tea in the great barn, and every year thereafter I hoped it would rain at precisely four o'clock so that we could enjoy the novelty all over again.

But subsequent years brought a fine hot day, when we had to stay under the trees in the shade and swing the whole afternoon till tea was ready on the lawn. Six swings were tied to the strongest branches of six giant oaks in the field nearest the house, but one was always commandeered by William and his friends, who liked to stand in pairs on the swing, shouting and showing off to the girls as they soared upwards into the branches.

The Superintendent, in the meantime, had opened his little tuckshop in a corner of the field, where we spent our pennies on lemonade, sherbet bags, aniseed balls, fruit drops, and chocolate.

When all the boxes were empty, and the last drop of lemonade drained from the cask, he closed the shop and pegged out the race course for the evening entertainment.

The boys' sack race was the best fun and the girls' egg and spoon the most serious—though all the eggs were solid china! Every child, no matter how young, slow, or awkward, had a chance of winning at least threepence, for the Superintendent and his two devoted sisters were so insistent on fair play, we felt quite guilty if we won more than sixpence!

As soon as the hop-picking season was over and the winter commenced, Miss Kate and Miss Ruth announced their plans for another concert—"in aid of those poor dear children of Dr. Barnardo." Rehearsals would start immediately and continue till January, every Tuesday evening at six o'clock in the chapel schoolroom.

We listened politely, and wondered whether we should be asked to sing solo or duet and who would recite the ever popular poem "Grace Darling." The Superintendent agreed to sing his usual boisterous rendering of "The Farmer's Boy," with "Widdicombe Fair" as an encore. Rehearsals went well, right from the start, though the boys gradually sneaked away to fight in the yard or climb up the drainpipes.

The little ones were persuaded once again "to sit

still and sing nicely, dear," while Miss Ruth played their favorite nursery rhymes on the wheezy little harmonium. "Action songs" by the younger girls always included "The Bells of St. Mary's" so that one of the few remaining boys could toll the school bell in the cloakroom.

That was followed by a "serious play" from the senior girls, in which the moral was always stressed by rather stilted dialogue, and Miss Kate, wringing her hands, would plead, "Girls! Girls! Do try to remember the action is taking place at a Band of Hope meeting, not at Widdicombe Fair!" I enjoyed these rehearsals, though I was always a little nervous of being "prevailed upon" to recite!

To my astonishment, one year I was asked to sing a solo with four long verses in costume, and I neither stuttered nor stopped dead in the middle from stage fright!

Miss Kate and Miss Ruth made all our costumes, and both had the patience of Job and untiring enthusiasm. We sold tickets for the concert—priced sixpence, ninepence, or a shilling—according to the generosity of the patrons.

Flushed and triumphant with success, we repeated the performance a second night for the benefit of "those poor dear children of Dr. Barnardo"—then, with many curtain calls and curtseys, retired from the limelight till next season.

Mother consulted William now on all matters of importance, and he was very conscious of his position as "man of the family" and elder brother. Gravely he tried to understand the many problems facing Mother, with a growing family and no father to provide for them.

"Are we poor?" he asked. "Really poor?"

Mother couldn't bear that word, so she hedged a little.

"We are not well off," she admitted.

"Did Father spend all his money, then?"

"Yes—all of it—but on us, on his family, and not on himself," she hastened to add.

"What are we going to do, then?" William frowned. "Gosh! I wish I was old enough to leave school, then I would earn pots of money—delivering papers and milk, and helping the gravedigger, and, well, all sorts of ways," he added manfully.

A wan smile flickered across Mother's anxious face. "Thank you, William, but it is your education that is my biggest worry. Boys must have a good education."

"And girls?" I ventured.

"Girls can manage better without too much learning, I believe. Anyway, it's rather wasted when they get married and have to spend the rest of their lives looking after homes and families."

I sighed. Always this great division between girls and boys.

"It's not fair!" I grumbled to myself as I sat down to mend a hole in my stocking.

But Mother was right—she was always right if only I could still persuade myself to believe it, as I had believed it without question when I was little and so profoundly trusting.

William was easily the most intelligent boy in the village school, and he had the highest marks in the scholarship for grammar school. Why, he might even go on to Oxford or Cambridge University later, where some of the Gentry finished their education. Then I should be the proudest girl in the whole world!

But William, who was concerned only with the immediate problem of making money, thoughtfully twirled a lock of hair while he considered the matter gravely.

"We could take a lodger." Mother suggested tentatively.

"A lodger?" scoffed William, as though it were some strange species of mankind. "Gosh, Mother, no! Anyway, we haven't got a spare room."

"We should have to arrange ourselves differently. The 'playroom' could be the lodger's bedroom. It's next door to the front room and has a separate door to the street. It's never been used much as a playroom, anyway. You all seemed to prefer to play in the kitchen when you were little, and you have always played outdoors, William, even in the winter," Mother pointed out. This was true. For some reason or other we hadn't cared much for the playroom.

"But what shall we do with a lodger? And is it a man or a woman?" William still looked doubtful.

"I don't know yet. I must make a few inquiries in the village. Perhaps the Vicar might suggest someone nice, though he was rather annoyed when we all changed over to chapel. Yes, I shall call on the Vicar to-morrow," Mother decided with renewed purpose. "The longer we postpone it, the harder it will be to adjust ourselves to change, for whoever it is, man or woman, must be made to feel 'at home,' you understand? The lodger will be included in everything from now on—just like one of the family."

William groaned, then marched out of the house in gloomy silence to tell his friend Richard that Mother was taking a lodger.

The following day, we waited impatiently for Mother at the vicarage gates. Then we saw her hurrying down the drive looking rather flushed.

"I've actually spoken to him on the telephone!" she exclaimed. "He's staying at the Railway Hotel. The lodger? Yes, of course I mean the lodger. And he sounds like a perfect gentleman!" she added with the greatest satisfaction.

We fired her with questions. What did he do? Where did he come from? What was his name? Had he any children? Should we have to call him "mister"? Was he an old man?

"Thirty? Gosh, that's old!" said William mournfully. who was expecting someone young enough to play marbles and leapfrog.

Mother told us all she knew as I laid the tea table and Mary made the toast.

Mr. John Martin was a young ex-officer—she still insisted he was young. He suffered from gas poisoning during the war, had several months in hospital, and was advised by the doctors to spend as much time as possible in the open air. So, instead of going back to London after the war, he had invested his money in a poultry farm. The farm was only two miles away, and he cycled there and back, and would come home to dinner "any time to suit my convenience, he told me in a most considerate way," Mother explained, and she looked very pleased and thought we were very lucky indeed to find such an agreeable young man to be our first lodger. Mr. Martin was not married, and he had only one sister, who spent most of her time abroad—"So he's practically an orphan, poor man," said Mother, already prepared to adopt him!

"And he likes children!" She sighed happily as she buttered the toast, and her face had lost its bleakness.

"Will he pay us, then, for living here?" asked William, who was anxious to get everything nicely settled financially.

"Thirty shillings a week," said Mother importantly.

"Thirty shillings?" William gulped. "That's a bit much, isn't it? Can he afford to pay all that money if he only looks after a few hens?"

"Hundreds, maybe thousands of hens," Mother explained. "And Mr. Martin himself suggested it. He says he will pay the same as he pays at the Railway Hotel, so that seems very fair to me. After all, I hadn't the vaguest idea what lodgers paid their landladies."

"Does that make you a landlady, then?" William looked doubtful again.

"Mother you c-c-can't!" I wailed. "The one at B-B-Brighton Station—"

"That's a lavatory lady, stupid!" William reminded me scornfully.

"We shall have to live carefully and not be at all extravagant, then we shall manage," Mother decided. "But I shall need some extra help from all of you with a lodger to look after as well as a family," she added.

We all agreed to her suggestion of regular Saturday jobs, though William was doubtful whether he could clean the knives—with red powder sprinkled on a board —*and* clean out the henhouse. After all, he had some very important things to do, and Saturday was supposed to be a holiday. But Mother was firm. "Duty first, then pleasure," she insisted.

"Pleasure? Who's talking of pleasure? I was thinking of something serious, like, well—electrical engineering, and suchlike," said William importantly, "but it's
to be a surprise."

"Electrical engineering?" gasped Mother, looking
extremely worried. "But we haven't even got gas? Oh,
William, do be careful. Is it dangerous?"

"Safe as houses!" he assured her. "But only me and
Richard know about it yet. We have to do a few more
experiments in his father's workshop, and, of course, we
haven't really got the proper equipment or the proper
tools." He sighed.

"Do be careful, William!" Mother called after him
as he went out to join Richard. "Oh, well, I suppose boys
will be boys," she told me resignedly. "Now, let's get
you two girls settled."

Mary could take over drying the dishes, and the
dusting on Saturday mornings, while I could make beds,
polish the brass knobs and clean the doorsteps with
squares of white hearthstone. A horrid job! I pulled a
face, and Mother pretended not to notice my total lack
of enthusiasm, and found a job for Henry. He could feed
and water the canary every day and clean out the cage
on Saturday.

With a little help from all of us, Mother had the
lodger's room ready by Monday, when Mr. Martin was
expected. It smelled strongly of soap and polish, and we
all had been robbed of something to make the lodger
comfortable. Mother had to manage with only two
blankets on her bed. William had to spare a pillow, very
reluctantly. Henry's counterpane was whisked away,
and he was most annoyed. Mary found her bedside chair
had disappeared, and she had only a screw on which to
hang her clothes.

"I don't mind," she said complacently.

But I was really indignant when I discovered the pretty flowered curtains in my bedroom had been replaced by unbleached calico. Why couldn't the lodger have calico curtains? Mother reminded me again that he was paying thirty shillings a week and must have the best.

A small rug was scooped off the landing, and one of the neighbors provided a secondhand bed and mattress. Mother insisted on a small payment of ten shillings, however. The front room had been robbed of a small occasional table, and a spare washstand was recovered from the box room.

The lemonade jug wreathed in roses was brought back into service again, and Mother exchanged a cracked basin for an uncracked basin—also from her bedroom. The lodger, being a "perfect gentleman," could not be expected to wash in a cracked basin, and we all must be ready and willing to "make do" and not make such a fuss about everything, she insisted.

Then we felt a little ashamed of our reluctance to part with familiar objects, and promised to be more co-operative in future. My good intentions lasted only a few days, however—I was ashamed to be seen cleaning the doorsteps on Saturday morning. Supposing any of my friends pass by? I should die! Mother reminded me again that I was getting very proud and stuck up and such humble tasks were not to be despised. Had I forgotten Mary in the Bible, who brought a bowl of water and a towel to wash the feet of Jesus when they were dirty and dusty from a long journey?

No, I hadn't forgotten Mary—but she hadn't to clean messy doorsteps, and anyway, Jesus never had dirty feet, because he paddled a lot in the Sea of Galilee!

"That's quite enough, thank you, Sarah. Now you are talking blasphemy!" she warned me.

So I crept out with a bucket early in the morning before breakfast, glanced furtively up and down the street, and whitened the doorsteps, in one of my most rebellious moods.

It was shameful enough to be seen kneeling on the pavement with a wet rag when the postman called. But when the Vicar rode by on his bicycle to take early Communion, my shame was so overwhelming, I kicked over the bucket and burst into tears.

William spent all Saturday morning making up his mind to clean the knives and the henhouse, and all Saturday afternoon watching his friend Richard doing it.

"There's nothing to it," said the patient, practical Richard—smeared in red powder and plastered with muck. "After all, somebody has to do it."

A pleasant freckled-faced man with a lot of straw-colored hair was sitting in the kitchen drinking tea with Mother when we came home from school on that eventful Monday.

He stood up, with a shy smile, to shake hands with us—Mother was right, he was a perfect gentleman! He was tall and lanky, and so terribly thin that his jacket and breeches hung flat to his body without shape.

Mother introduced us in the correct manner, and we all murmured, "Good afternoon, Mr. Martin," and stood there shyly and uncomfortably.

Our new lodger, equally shy and uncomfortable, gave a little nervous cough and suggested that we might like to call him "Uncle," since Mr. Martin was a little formal.

"I should like it immensely, because, unfortunately, I have no nieces and nephews and have never yet had the privilege of being an uncle."

Again that hesitant smile made us feel we were going to like this tall, gawky stranger, in spite of our intentions not to like him.

"Do you approve of the children calling me 'Uncle'?" he asked with polite deference, and Mother looked pleased and said she certainly approved, and the children would call him "Uncle John."

I was surprised to find Henry smiling at the stranger, and Mary was quite friendly, too, and offered to fetch his slippers. But Mother never called her lodger anything else than "Mr. Martin" for over five years.

And he, in turn, respecting her conventional standards of respectability, always stood up when she entered the room, and always behaved like the perfect gentleman he was meant to be.

So a new chapter of our lives began, in which this quiet, gentle, cultured man became so much a part of the family we could not imagine life without him.

When neither Mother nor teacher could give us a really satisfactory answer, William and I would say confidently, "Let's ask Uncle John—he'll know."

We regarded him as a sort of human encyclopedia, and even William was impressed by his profound wisdom!

Perhaps we had expected the lodger to be bold and boastful, but he was neither bold nor boastful, but stepped so quietly and unobtrusively into our lives, we felt no disturbing influences at all. Seven days a week, in breeches, jacket, and rubber boots, he waved us good-bye after an early breakfast and went off on his bicycle to look after his chickens.

He was the most completely contented person I had ever known.

After a few months, I noticed that William, quite unconsciously, was copying Uncle John's behavior. He became more polite and less aggressive, and his few uncontrollable fits of temper were followed by swift apologies. This could only be example, Mother contended, for her lodger had never once interfered with her upbringing—never once scolded or complained about rudeness, naughtiness, or disobedience, and, indeed, seemed to be oblivious of any misdemeanor.

Was it because he treated William as an adult that he gradually responded to the quiet stranger, yet had so resented his own father?

Why did Henry climb on his knee of his own free will, and Mary offer to make his toast or to fetch his *Daily Telegraph?*

Why did I hurry home from school with some fresh problem to be solved, or some new word I had discovered?

Because we trusted him? Because we liked him?

Or because he was such a "perfect gentleman"?

For me, it was a mixture of all three. For "gentleman" was not "Gentry," as I had supposed, for Uncle John was not one of their set. He was well bred, educated, cultured—and a gentleman. They were arrogant, proud, condescending—and *Gentry!*

I suppose I liked him for another good reason. He was such a good listener, and I was still such a poor conversationalist, with long pauses and much stuttering.

He did not remind me to speak slowly or start again or look uncomfortable while I blushed and stammered, but he sat quietly smoking a pipe, waiting for me to continue in my own way.

Because I was so crazy about words, he bought me a dictionary for my eleventh birthday, so that I could find the correct definitions and not just make a wild guess.

William was the first to discover Uncle John's poultry farm one Saturday morning, because he was now allowed to ride the beautiful new bicycle that was given to Mother—to cycle to his new school four miles away. She had sold Father's bicycle for ten pounds on the advice of her lodger to one of his customers, and bought a Valor Perfection oil stove for cooking in the summer months, and also a ton of coal! It overflowed from the coal shed into the back yard, and we all went out to inspect it, for usually our coal was delivered in two, not twenty, hundredweights!

William came back to report there were millions of chickens and masses of eggs. He was very impressed by Uncle John's management and industry, and decided to be a poultry farmer.

The electrical engineering phase had been short-lived, after the two boys, William and Richard, had spent all one wet and windy Saturday taking yards of wire flex up the stairs and around Mother's bedroom. She went to bed that night in the faint gleam of a single tiny bulb, borrowed from the cycle lamp and glowing in the darkness over her bed like a distant glowworm!

William had been a Boy Scout now for two years and had even been to camp. So after my eleventh birthday I was allowed to join the Girl Guides, and Mary joined the Brownies. Since nothing was made easy for us, we now had to walk the two miles to the poultry farm, and back, every Saturday afternoon to collect eggs and help with packing and feeding—to earn some extra pocket money, to buy our uniforms. The spoiling we had known for that brief period of our lives was not repeated, and sometimes I longed for that warm-hearted father with his fierce hugs and kisses—and that strong shoulder to cry on.

When Mother took a lodger, I was terribly afraid that he would take Father's place. But now I was no longer afraid, for I realized this would never happen.

6
The Aunties

Grandmother Prior, who eloped with a poor farmer at the age of seventeen and was left a widow at thirty-five, had eight children—two boys and six girls. The boys, William and Henry, lived just long enough to bequeath their names to my two brothers, then quietly died—of measles.

Grandmother Prior was still a very remarkable and distinctive old lady, with piercing blue eyes and a noble head on which she piled her richly abundant hair—white as snow and soft as thistledown—with an assortment of tortoiseshell combs. She dressed elegantly, and always in black, apart from white lace ruffles at the neck and sleeves.

And, unlike her daughters, she had a passion for jewelry. Long strings of pearls, brooches, rings, bracelets, and watches filled a satin-lined box on her dressing table and spilled over in sparkling profusion onto a slender glass tray.

It seemed that Grandmother Prior was still in mourning, thirty years later, for the poor struggling young farmer who had become even poorer and given up the struggle altogether after the birth of their eighth and last child. Yet one felt instinctively that Grandmother, with her proud dignity and strong personality, would never have given up the struggle.

In the summer, Grandmother Prior strolled along the promenade, with a parasol shading her delicate skin from the hot rays of the sun. In winter, she always carried a rolled umbrella with an ebony handle shaped like a parrot.

Our mother, who was Grandmother Prior's eldest daughter, had inherited her proud dignity and strong character, but also the dark eyes and olive skin of her father.

If they wept at all, these two strong-willed women, they wept in the privacy of their bedrooms and not in public. We never saw their tears, but neither did we know their laughter, though both, we were told, had been gay in their youth.

To walk with Grandmother Prior down the village street on the splendid occasion of her visit to Kent was to walk with Royalty.

It was a proud privilege, not to be indulged in lightly, and necessitated the wearing of Sunday best, including hat and gloves, even on a Saturday. William was so impressed by his grandmother's stately dignity, he forsook the river, the fish, and the birds, and deserted his bosom friend Richard in order to escort her to the draper's, where she purchased only one small item: a pale mauve veil to drape her fashionable straw hat and fall prettily over her hair and eyes.

She had tiny hands and feet, and wore dainty little button boots that she polished every day with a silk handkerchief. Seeing her so fastidious in old age, it was difficult to imagine her as a farmer's wife in her youth. She must have loved her young farmer very dearly to exchange a luxurious home in London in which, as an adored only child, she enjoyed many privileges, including a private governess, music and dancing lessons, and the sheltered seclusion of a well-bred young lady.

Perhaps she was too sheltered?

But where did she meet her young farmer if she always had an escort or a chaperone?

How and where did this romance begin? I wanted to know, for the story thrilled and intrigued me. But Mother was extremely reticent on the matter of the elopement, and these vital questions still remain unanswered.

To ask Grandmother Prior personally would have seemed both rude and impertinent, for children were not encouraged to delve into the private world of adults.

"It was not our business"—"It did not concern us" were the answers we received.

But always I thought of Grandmother Prior in a romantic, not a practical, way and indulged my fancy in imaginative scenes in which a beautiful young girl looking exactly like Juliet was carried down a rope ladder by a handsome Romeo. In reality, however, it may have been quite a mundane affair, and the young farmer may have been delivering fresh butter and cream or poultry to one of his well-to-do customers in the city.

Perhaps he seduced her? Or she seduced him? We shall never know. The chapter is closed forever.

The Aunties—Sarah, Emily, Amelia, Harriet, and Mary—had much of their mother's dignity, but not her distinction.

Their personalities, even as adults, always seemed a little overshadowed by this proud, self-willed old lady, who had at last inherited the imposing residence known as "The Retreat"—her late father's seaside house at Worthing. Her five daughters, all unmarried, shared this house with their mother for many years, living modestly on the interest of great-grandfather's capital investments.

We heard mention of Stocks and Shares, Railways, Breweries, and Coal—and a family solicitor who apparently knew everything and from whom no secrets were hid.

The youngest Auntie—nicknamed "the Auntie who smells nice" because of her passion for Icilma—also indulged in romantic daydreams, and once divulged the secret of the family finances.

Great-grandfather, it seemed, had never forgiven his runaway daughter, and consequently left a will in which she was disinherited—apart from the seaside house and the interest on his very considerable fortune.

As a child, it all seemed very involved, unkind, and unnecessary. I told Mother I hated this autocratic great-grandfather who dared to shut his only daughter out of the Kingdom of Heaven.

She looked at me in some bewilderment.

"But what has Heaven to do with it?" she asked.

"Nothing—but it s-s-sounds nice!" I told her enigmatically.

From my earliest recollections, we went to visit Grandmother Prior and the Aunties once a year, at

Whitsuntide. It was the highlight of our year—an exciting and enviable excursion into another world, to be talked about, and greatly exaggerated—by me—on our return.

Apart from "the Auntie who smells nice" we were met at the station by "the strict Auntie," "the kind Auntie," "the swanky Auntie," and "the Auntie who likes the beach."

After our perilous journey by train, involving two changes, at Tunbridge Wells and Brighton, we arrived hot and exhausted in all our Sunday best regalia to greet the Aunties shyly and politely on the station platform.

William by this time was ready and relieved to hand me over to anyone, no matter who.

He was sick to death of escorting a tiresome young sister with no sense of direction and an avid curiosity. Brighton Station was the limit of his endurance, he told Mother, and, in future, if I dared to make one more stupid remark about it being the biggest village in the world, he would push me under a train!

Poor Mother! This annual excursion to the seaside was no picnic for her, either, with four young children, a pile of luggage, and a pram to supervise.

She always looked a little vexed and jaded at the end of the journey, but her tired face relaxed into a joyful smile of welcome, seeing her five sisters, all looking graciously dignified (and all wearing hats and gloves, though only five minutes' walk from home), clustered together on the platform.

I was always much impressed and flattered by our welcome, for none of the other travelers alighting from the train could boast more than two people come to meet them.

We were kissed rather hurriedly, because "lunch was ready, and Grandmother mustn't be kept waiting." Then we bustled down the street, with a porter trailing us with our baggage on a trolley.

Grandmother met us in the hall with a disarming smile and a delicate peck of a kiss; and I looked about me, starry-eyed with excitement. This was where I belonged, I told myself importantly—not in that poky little cottage, with its brick floors and damp walls. But in this beautiful, spacious, richly furnished house, where even the cat sat on a cushion.

I begged to be allowed to look at everything now, this very minute.

"After lunch dear," said Grandmother, so I had to be content with that.

The grandeur of the dining room so impressed me on my first day, I could only nibble at the food.

Even with Grandmother, five Aunties, Mother and her four children seated at the table, there seemed to be room for several more.

The solid Jacobean furniture in this room was highly polished, the starched linen tablecloth and napkins immaculately white, the silver gleaming, the dinner service of willow pattern design, complete with two tureens, one for gravy and the other for mint sauce. The roast lamb was succulent, and my favorite trifle sprinkled with coconut, but I was choked with excitement and impatient for the long meal to end so that I could explore every inch of the house with a rapture that never faded throughout my childhood.

We children sat quietly, spread out between the Aunties, listening shyly to the six sisters talking of this and that, and catching Grandmother's smile at the head of the table.

But we had to wait for her permission to leave the table.

Mary and Henry, perched on cushions on either side of Mother, were too shy to speak a word at the first meal other than "Yes, please," or "No, thank you," and that was compulsory.

William would be gravely polite and pass the salt to everyone within reach. Then Grandmother Prior, proudly erect in her high-backed Jacobean chair, would bend her head to say Grace. "For what we have received may the Lord make us truly thankful. Amen."

"Have you forgotten, child, you remove your shoes before you enter the drawing room?"

It was the tart voice of the strict Auntie behind me as I hovered on the threshold, and I jumped out of my skin, for I had forgotten.

Mother said it was unkind to give Auntie Sarah this particular nickname, because she had a "heart of gold" hidden away inside, and also she had made so many of our clothes since we were born. The sharp voice was just a disguise to hide her real feelings, Mother insisted, as some people wore a mask to hide their faces at a carnival.

I promised to remember this in future, but I always forgot, and every year it was the same, and her voice made me jump out of my skin and blush guiltily.

But when she stood beside me on the threshold and was satisfied that I held my shoes in my hand, she said kindly, "You may come in here, child, whenever you wish, in your stockinged feet."

I thanked her, and we smiled at each other tentatively, for a year is a long time, and we were both shy.

The Aunties

Because she was my godmother and had given me her name, I had received a Bible and a prayer book on my eighth and ninth birthday, inscribed, "To my Goddaughter Sarah, from her loving Godmother."

But we were never quite sure if she really liked children, for her heart of gold was covered in prickles. I think William was her favorite, and he was not afraid of her. She fussed over him like a mother hen with a chick and followed him around asking stilted questions about his education, his hobbies, and his friends—and dusting off imaginary dust from his collar. The Aunties, it seems, had taken one peep at their first nephew in his pram and decided to call him "Boy."

In a way, I suppose, it was a compliment to the solemn dark-eyed child, for nobody had ever to peep in the pram and ask, "Is it a boy or a girl?" as we did with the neighbors. "William was never a baby, but always a boy," Mother would say proudly of her first-born.

The drawing room was used only for such purposes as entertaining the Vicar to afternoon tea, or for Grandmother to play a little Chopin on the rosewood piano, with its pink quilted frontispiece.

The white sheepskin rugs curled around my stockinged feet as I tiptoed across the room to the conservatory. Queen Anne chairs were placed at precise angles, and all were draped in rose-patterned chintz, with elaborate cushions, embroidered and tasseled.

Oil paintings in heavy gilt frames decorated the walls, and several occasional tables held china ornaments and photographs in silver frames.

Delicately I stepped between the chairs and the occasional tables, drawing deep satisfying breaths of that peculiar and very special smell that belonged there. It was neither musty nor fresh, but had in it a faint suggestion of lavender and old lace, and a lovely old-fashioned melody seemed to linger in the room, so that I half-expected to see Great-grandmother in a crinoline.

Each room had its own special smell, even the conservatory.

When I opened the door and went in, the hot air licked my face, and the warm scent of geraniums was overwhelmingly sweet. In a corner, on the floor, I rediscovered our buckets and spades, little boats, and two old tennis balls—for playing in the park till the Auntie who liked the beach was ready for us.

Every year the tin buckets looked a little more shabby, then they lost their handles, and finally leaked. Then, and only then, were they replaced by new ones.

The balls were threadbare and soggy, and very poor bouncers, but we had to "make do" with them. We all hated this enforced period of playing in the park after breakfast—often for an hour or more—and we would toss the balls listlessly across the grass for ten minutes and then stand expectantly at the park gates waiting to be collected.

The breakfast room was not used for breakfast any more, but as a sewing room, and here the Aunties made all our clothes, and their own clothes. The smell of singed cloth lingered in the room from the hot iron.

The hall, with its stained-glass window, sometimes smelled of wet mackintoshes and umbrellas. A little green gate in the hall led to the basement kitchen and scullery and the Aunties' breakfast room. Grandmother always had her breakfast in bed.

The basement stairs were dark, and the smell of gas always lingered there. Auntie Amelia—the kind

Auntie—did all the cooking and washing up and spent most of her time in the basement. She was a big, strong, rather masculine woman and always good-tempered and happy. She had, however, one shocking habit that was so shocking it was called a vice—she *smoked.*

All her sisters in turn had tried to stop her, especially Sarah, who was so shocked whenever she saw a faint glow of a cigarette, she nearly swooned.

But Amelia, in this one respect, was quite incorrigible and continued to smoke in a secretive way for years in the basement. Sometimes a faint whiff of tobacco smoke would drift up the basement stairs, and Sarah or Harriet or Emily would give a little scream and fan the air with their handkerchiefs and open all the windows to air the place.

The bedroom we shared with three of the Aunties was like a school dormitory, with six beds and two sofas. Bunches of purple wisteria draped the outside walls and windows like bunches of purple grapes.

Fascinated by the splendor of gaslight and a lavatory with a chain to pull, we often asked to "be excused" in the middle of the night!

The two youngest Aunties—Harriet and Mary—were rather privileged, and spoiled, with bedrooms of their own and suitors calling regularly.

They both went out to business at rather select houses of fashion in the town. Auntie Mary—the Auntie who smells nice—was very fair, with pink cheeks and blue eyes. She was often in a daydream and seemed not to notice we were there. We hoped her suitors liked Icilma and listening to the band, for this was her favorite pastime on summer evenings.

Auntie Harriet—the swanky Auntie—was dark and

vivacious. She seemed to have more temperament, more suitors, and more of everything than the others.

At one time, no less than three suitors were courting her, on different days, in different ways—but you shall hear in a later chapter how she rejected all three for someone else.

Grandmother loved little girls, and she told us so repeatedly as we stood at her knee reciting our little verses, or sat on hassocks beside her while she played our favorite hymns—on the dining-room, not the drawing-room piano. She still had a sweet though rather quavery voice that joined our shrill discordant voices in a most unharmonious way. But we liked to think we were rather specially favored by Grandmother, Mary and I, and allowed to enjoy certain privileges the boys were denied. We joined her in bed, at precisely seven-thirty, for early morning tea.

While the two youngest Aunties remained in bed and had tea delivered to their rooms (*"We* go out to business" was their excuse to be relieved of such humdrum duties), the others had to take turns to make the tea.

We would hear them arguing—"It's your turn, Emily. I did it last week." And Emily would "turn nasty" and insist it was Sarah's turn. Finally Amelia would decide to do it again—"just for this once"—and they would let her do it, knowing her sweet unselfish nature.

Climbing up two long flights of stairs with a tray from the basement was no easy task, and we would watch anxiously from above, hanging over the banisters.

Tapping politely on the door, we waited on the threshold to be invited to enter Grandmother's bedroom.

This room also had its own particular smell, associated only with Grandmother and nobody else. It was a mixture of lavender water, scented soap, and liniment, together with a warm scented stuffiness that made the Aunties wrinkle their noses, for they all were rather fond of fresh air. Grandmother Prior was not at all fond of fresh air—perhaps she had too much of it in her youth on that remote farmstead in Surrey? Now, in her declining years, she indulged her fancy for warmth and stuffiness, and would often have a fire in her bedroom and all the windows closed.

Her bed was luxuriously soft and downy, and she would be wearing a pretty shawl draped around her shoulders. Her dimpled cheeks were pink as a baby's, and we kissed her gently and waited for our tea and biscuits.

If it was Auntie Sarah's turn, she covered us in towels first, and Auntie Emily brought bibs, but dear Auntie Amelia, who had more turns to make the tea than anyone else, would smile benignly and probably trip over a hassock or a slipper and slop the tea in the saucers. This always made us giggle, and Grandmother's eyes would twinkle as she passed us the biscuit tin. It was the biscuit that was the real highlight of early morning tea with Grandmother—a plain petit-buerre biscuit. This to me was the very essence of extravagant living—early morning tea and a biscuit.

To this day, a plain petit-buerre biscuit holds nostalgic memories of Grandmother and her soft, luxurious bed.

Then we drifted in and out of the other bedrooms, watching the Aunties brushing their hair, though we were not allowed in until they had reached the petticoat and camisole stage of dressing. It was too indelicate, and they were too modest.

The swanky Auntie would take ages deciding what to wear, then try on several hats and reject them all in favor of a bright scarlet beret she wore at a jaunty angle. This made people stare, and some would ask if she came from Paris. In her fashionable dress and the scarlet beret, she certainly looked more like a Parisian than Mother's sister. She always wore bright colors—scarlet, emerald green, or daffodil yellow. Her black hair was cut in a boyish bob that suited her well, and if she had shocked her family of sisters by cutting her hair, she wouldn't care, for she liked shocking people. We found her startling dress and her variable moods rather disconcerting. Children amused her sometimes, but not often; and when her suitors called at the house, we were told to run away and play. Her bedroom was always untidy, because she was always in a hurry and changed her clothes so often she had no time to put them away. She used an expensive French perfume that lingered in the room all day.

As I grew older, I envied her, not only the French perfume and her fashionable clothes—she never wore homemade clothes—but also her dashing devil-may-care attitude that set her apart from her more conventional sisters and attracted several suitors. This, I felt, was the very essence of womanly attribute—while I was shy, gauche, and stuttering.

To bathe in the sea was a major operation. The Aunties paid strict adherence to "modesty," and whether you were four or fourteen, only legs were allowed to be seen naked.

Our bathing costumes, stored carefully in a drawer in the sewing room, sometimes attracted moths, and we found a number of little holes that had to be patched or darned. Every year they appeared a little more faded and a little more difficult to squeeze into, for they were "handed down" and shrunk. Nothing was wasted or rejected as too old for use, and even the tea towels were patched. The Aunties, in an atmosphere of genteel respectability, were "making do" on a modest income that did not allow for a servant—though servants were cheap and plentiful.

Great-grandfather had servants, both at his town and seaside houses, but when he died, they packed their boxes and left, with a small pension for services rendered.

Getting into the sea was a fairly straightforward operation, for everything was still dry, but it was coming out I dreaded so much. Shivering and dripping wet, I had to wait for Henry and then Mary to be dried first under the bath towel tent fixed to the breakwater; for Auntie Emily could not cope with more than one child at a time, and it was always "youngest first" or "ladies first" with the Aunties. I was not even fond of bathing, but I had to pretend to like it, because you were considered a little odd if you spent a seaside holiday just paddling and messing about in pools. Besides, I had to swank about my marvelous bathes to my friends in the village, who never had seaside holidays.

"Careful, dear! Cover yourself!" Auntie Emily would whisper hoarsely through a gap in the tent, while I fought and struggled to remove the horrid clammy garment clinging to my ribs. It was usually sticky with seaweed and gritty with sand.

"Try to stand up, dear, then I can put my hand through here and dry your back," prompted a patient voice from outside.

But I was always a long time, and William was furious with me because he, too, was waiting his turn with chattering teeth. "Buck up, Sarah! Do you hear me? Gosh! You're as slow as a snail."

This urged me on to greater efforts, but my vest got stuck on my damp shoulders, and my knickers clung to my thighs like gummed paper.

"Come on! I'm frozen!" wailed William every two seconds or so, for he was not accustomed to be kept waiting by his sisters and younger brother. Then he demanded that I come out—or else—so I crept out, damp and shivering, and looking rather like a bedraggled mermaid with my long wet hair. We always wore bathing caps, Mary and I, but I never learned to swim—only to float, and the water poured in.

The remainder of the operation—a hot cup of tea from the flask, to be shared with Mary or Henry, and a brisk run along the promenade to get our circulation back—was quickly done. I was always glad to get it over for the day, then I could really begin to enjoy the seaside.

We saved our pocket money all the year—apart from the few shillings we spent at Christmas and for birthday presents, and the pennies at Mrs. Mercer's sweetshop.

Grandmother generously added another five shillings to each purse, and it seemed like a fortune we had to spend. We bought our ice creams from a man on the beach who carried a heavy box slung on his shoulder and called out, "Okey-pokey!" Why he called "okey-pokey" and not "ice-cream" we never discovered, but it didn't matter.

Mary and I spent most of our pocket money on riding in the goat carriages, until we were too big to squeeze inside, then we had to be content to watch Henry on the driver's seat.

We preferred to sit inside the carriage on the tiny cushioned seats, waving to everyone in the grandest style as we moved slowly and sedately the hundred yards or so to the bandstand and back. There were four little carriages, each drawn by two goats, and all were scrupulously spick and span—or we should not have been allowed to patronize them!

These goat carriages on the promenade were the biggest attraction for small children, and took more customers than Punch and Judy.

We had always to wait our turn for the privilege of riding in one of these carriages, but the seaside holiday only really started, for me when I sat with Mary in a little goat carriage, bowing and waving to everyone— like two Cinderellas in sun hats and sandals, with sea-weed in their hair.

We went back to the house for a midday lunch, and returned to the beach for the afternoon, taking a picnic tea.

Six days a week, the pattern of our seaside holiday varied only in detail—one day we would have Bath buns for tea, and another day sugar buns—one day we might indulge in two rides in a goat carriage and two ice creams! But we were content to have it so, and any suggestion of alternative entertainment met with cries of "But what about the beach?" Sometimes, but not often, the Aunties would be prevailed upon to join us for a picnic tea at four o'clock, when they sat sedately in full regalia on deck chairs, and only removed their gloves to nibble at a small sandwich or a tiny portion of Madeira cake (they always brought their own dainty teas).

We sat on the pebbles with Mother and the Auntie who liked the beach and ate ravenously of thick sandwiches and buns.

Auntie Emily always seemed like one of us, and we wondered why she had no children of her own, when she was so kind and sensible and rather like Mother. She never tired of us for the whole of the two weeks—but the others did. She was an outdoor person, and she loved to get up at the crack of dawn and cycle to the beach for a swim before breakfast—coming back to the house brisk and glowing to eat a large bowl of oatmeal porridge.

As we grew older, one by one we were allowed to join her on these early morning spartan exercises, and we rode off in a noisy contingent on borrowed bicycles.

The sea was even more vast and more alarming with no boats or bathers other than ourselves, and the journey back both chilly and uncomfortable, for we did not remove our clinging wet costumes, but covered ourselves in long cold Burberrys to ride home.

Water squelched in our canvas shoes and dripped from our hair as we pedaled along in a silent, shivering group, with Auntie Emily, pink and glowing from her swim, leading the procession.

But it was all part of the seaside holiday and couldn't be missed—for fear of William's scorn or Mother's anxious "Oh, Sarah, you haven't got another stomachache?"

And the Auntie who liked the beach would have been so surprised and disappointed had she known of my reluctance to bathe.

Six days a week we went to the beach, but Sunday was the Sabbath—holiday or not. Dressed in our Sunday best, we all assembled in the hall at precisely ten-thirty, to accompany Grandmother and the Aunties to church.

After church, we walked slowly and sedately along the promenade, glancing longingly at the beach and the little goat carriages.

A walk in the park in the afternoon (no balls allowed) was followed by a special Sunday tea that helped to compensate for the cold mutton and boiled potatoes earlier in the day. Then a quiet hour of hymn-singing and learning texts from the Bible, still in the dining room, because of the awful possibility of soiling a drawing-room chair.

Yet I truthfully enjoyed these two Sundays we spent in this quiet way, for they, too, were part of the holiday, and part of the charm and dignity of Grandmother's way of life.

William and Henry, who found the Sundays both long and tedious, were sulky and bad-tempered by evening. But Mary and I, perhaps because we both loved dressing up in our Sunday best, enjoyed walking out with Grandmother and all Mother's sisters, and especially going to church, where we received many admiring glances as we filed into two pews in the center aisle.

We also enjoyed having our long hair unloosened from weekday plaits and hanging in curls, with "Alice bands" or bows of ribbon to add to the glory of our beautiful tresses.

One never-to-be-forgotten Sunday evening, William was so overcome by boredom—he was probably about ten years of age at the time—that he was rude to Grandmother.

Mother was horrified and the Aunties shocked. It was unpardonable, they said, and must not go unpunished. Mary and I begged for his forgiveness, since William himself was too proud to beg.

We went to bed early and wondered what form the punishment would take. The next morning, we started out for the beach, and William was missing. My heart missed a beat, and I refused to move another step until he had been found or some explanation was forthcoming.

Then I saw his face at the bedroom window, pale and tense, but still defiant. He had not and would not apologize, Mother told us anxiously, so he had been ordered to remain in the bedroom.

Mary and I, both sobbing hysterically, were dragged off to the beach with Henry. We accused Mother and Auntie Emily of cruelty and wickedness, and made ourselves so unpleasant they were glad to drag us home again—still crying in sympathy for William.

We found him still in the bedroom, but somebody had taken him cocoa and biscuits and a book to read. Was it the kind Auntie? Nobody knew, and William was dumb.

Still he hadn't apologized by teatime, and now everyone was in such a nervous state—all except William, who was lying on the bed reading *Robinson Crusoe* from cover to cover—that it became doubtful whether the crime was so serious after all.

Grandmother, who had taken very little part in the punishment and its most unhappy consequences, was surprised to discover William on his bed in the middle of the afternoon.

"My dear, are you ill?" she inquired anxiously. "Would you like me to get my smelling salts?"

"No, thank you, Grandmother," said William politely, with one of his rare angelic smiles. "You see, I am not ill. I was rude."

"Oh, but I'm sure you didn't mean to be rude, dear boy," said Grandmother soothingly, thinking what a handsome little boy he was, and so much like her dear departed Matthew.

Then she kissed his brow, stroked his dark head, and invited him down to tea.

"And what would you like, my dear, toasted muffins?" she was asking as they came downstairs hand in hand a few minutes later.

Going home by train at the end of the holiday, Mary and I flattened our noses against the windowpane and howled. The cottage seemed mean and poor and terribly small, the rooms damp and dreary. We hated it.

"It's because you *compare* everything, Sarah. Grandmother's house is not really so grand, and our cottage not so terribly small. Anyhow, it is Home," said Mother sensibly as she started to unpack. "Tomorrow it will be all right again, you'll see. Now, stop crying and drink up your cocoa, there's a good girl."

7
Friends and Neighbors

"She's getting like her father," the neighbors said of me now. And my friends gave me new names, like "Cocky" and "Perky" and "Sarah Sharp."

William found a new word, "bumptious," when he suddenly discovered I had a will as strong as his own.

Mother was alternately distressed and annoyed, for I changed, almost overnight—not from an ugly duckling into a swan, but from a shy, fanciful creature into this bouncy, confident girl, with a loud laugh, a strutting walk, and a wild desire to hug everyone within reach.

No wonder they said of me, "She's getting like her father." But I hadn't his flaming red hair or flaming temper, and I was not copying him or anyone else—I just wanted to be myself.

For seven years or more, I had stuttered and been made utterly miserable by this strange handicap that was thrust upon me at the age of six by the sudden impact with a teacher who practiced sadism in a class of small defenseless children.

The invisible cord that tied my tongue for so long gradually loosened as I grew into adolescence and began to shed my haunting childish fears, nightmares, and sleepwalking.

Mother was right, she was always right. I did grow out of it, and only because of her practical common sense and her most exemplary example. Self-pity was discouraged. Self-discipline practiced constantly.

But I didn't grow out of the stomachache. Now the ache was a horrible sickening pain, more frequent and more frightening, and I spent more days on the sofa. Dr. Bird was called in to examine my queer protruding stomach. Like Mother, he thought I should grow out of it and prescribed a large dose of castor oil, for which I hated him ever after.

Uncle John was a great comfort at these times, and he would read to me when he came home in the evening, and we would pore over the dictionary and the atlas, searching for new words and new worlds to conquer. He helped me to learn the theory part of first aid for my Girl Guide badge, and also the practical part, by pretending he had fractured a leg or broken his ankle or dislocated his shoulder.

Mother was worried that her lodger might get tired of her children's demands on his time, but she needn't have worried, for we knew that his interest was genuine and that he really cared about us.

The caring was mutual, for we all liked him and

depended on him—not as a second father, but more as an elder brother.

He taught me to ride Mother's bicycle, for now we three younger children had to share it, and William had one of his own he had bought secondhand with the money he earned delivering early morning papers.

I soon learned to carry Mary or Henry on the carrier, and we would travel at break-neck speed down the steep hills to the poultry farm on Saturday afternoons— and then have to push it all the way back.

Neither Mary nor Henry cared much for this uncomfortable means of transport and would hug me around the waist, imploring me not to go so fast, but this was just another opportunity to show off, and I made good use of it!

My life now had suddenly become a feverish endeavor to catch up on the days I lost lying on the sofa. When I was well, I was boisterously well; and when I was sick, I was near to dying—or so I imagined. Now I had to cram into my "good days" all my schooling, friends, housecraft, Girl Guides, chapel, concert practice, Band of Hope, nature study, writing stories and verse, reading, and packing eggs for Uncle John to make up for my "bad days" on the sofa.

Since I could not bear to miss anything or give up anything, I usually spent the first hour on the sofa in floods of tears, bewailing the fact that I was going to miss my favorite composition lesson with my darling Miss Harvey, or my chance to lead my Swallow Patrol to victory, or my choir practice, or tea with my friend Elsie Partridge, or my turn to make the shepherd's pie at the Housecraft Center, or going to chapel in my Sunday best, or joining in those heartwarming choruses at

Band of Hope. I cried with pain and frustration, then I cried because I wanted a shoulder to cry on.

Mother left me alone—to get over it. Then she brought me a nice cup of tea and a sponge cake, the current issue of the *Children's Newspaper*, an exercise book, and a pencil.

"Try to forget the stomachache, Sarah, there's a good girl. Write something," she suggested vaguely, for she had a poor opinion of all my scribbling, and she thought I could be more usefully occupied with knitting. It was a soothing occupation, she said, and good for the nerves.

"I hate knitting, and it's not at all soothing. It makes me want to scream!" I told her. She sighed, looked at my tongue, prodded my pickaninny stomach, and went away.

But I was worried about my figure. I was thirteen now and as flat and shapeless as a child of nine or ten— apart from the stomach.

Now I prayed passionately to wake up one morning to find I had breasts. All my friends had breasts.

It was most humiliating.

One of my best friends had a family so different from ours, I was constantly shocked and surprised by them. In a sprawling old cottage were crowded Elsie's parents, two married sisters, four brothers, and several young children. All through the years they always had a baby, and at one time the youngest Partridge was uncle to a baby who shared his pram.

The girls had a Romany beauty and were bold and merry.

The boys were big and strong and fond of teasing. I was a little afraid of them.

Lines of wet nappies flapped in the yard, and a little enamel chamber pot always stood ready for use on the fender. There were no weaklings in the Partridge family, and their babies seemed stronger and heavier to hold than other people's babies—even Henry could not have competed with a young Partridge.

Into this noisy happy-go-lucky family I was often invited by Elsie, who had only to fling open the door and bawl at the top of her voice, "Ma! I brought Sarah to tea." It was as simple as that. Everyone was welcome. Keys were never used and doors never locked. Food was plentiful, and the tablecloth stayed on the kitchen table all day. If you were late for tea, you were just in time for supper.

In winter, it would be fried fish and chips or sausages and mash. In summer, veal and ham pie and salad. A large jar of pickled onions would be handed around, and they all would make great play jabbing the onions with their forks, while the baby sucked the vinegary fingers with great relish.

Mother called it "an open house," and was careful to warn me of the pitfalls of such a careless and carefree way of life. One should have principles and purpose, orderliness and discipline, all of which were sadly lacking in the Partridges.

"But I like them, Mother. I think they are a lovely family, and they are always happy," I reminded her.

Louise and Lottie Sands also came into this category of my best friends, and they were extremely genteel, with parents who liked to keep themselves to themselves.

The two girls were permitted to join the Girl

Guides, but not until their parents were satisfied that the rest of us were nice respectable girls. This was their only diversion, and they certainly made the most of it, for usually they were expected to join their parents on quiet walks in the country with a quiet dog.

They lived in quite a pretentious type of villa, with lace curtains draping all the windows and an aspidistra in the hall. Everything about them was neat and formal and very discreet.

Twice a year, on their birthdays, I was invited to tea, with only two other girls. It was deemed a privilege, and I was greatly honored to be one of the chosen few.

We wore our Sunday best, ate daintily of thin bread and butter and raspberry jam and a cake with pink sugar icing. Then we played quietly with their dolls and inspected their wardrobes, for they were very clothes-conscious and always beautifully dressed.

They both asked to join the Swallow Patrol, so that made four of us.

Number five was a tomboy with red-gold hair and an impish grin. She was very popular, and we could always depend on Patsy to support our valiant efforts to win back the coveted trophy from the Robins or the Thrushes. She could tie the quickest sheepshank and run the fastest in relay, and her energy and enthusiasm were most infectious. We called her "a good sport." I was the leader of the Swallow Patrol and Patsy my second in command. Sometimes she would link her arm in mine and tell me, "I'm going to ask my mum if you can come to tea today, and she's sure to say yes, because she likes you, Sarah!"

Fishing for compliments, I would ask, "Why does your mother like me?"

A Village Girl

And Patsy, giving my arm an affectionate squeeze, would reply vaguely, "I dunno—she just does."

Number six was a timid little girl who had to be sheltered and protected. Her name was Evangeline, and she was the only child of elderly parents, who had been surprised and shocked to discover themselves parents at middle-age. Poor little Evangeline grew up in a timid, apologetic sort of way, and she always had to wear layers of clothes in case she caught cold.

She was allowed to ask just one friend on her birthday, and chose me for several years.

I was sorry for Evangeline, but more sorry for myself, as we sat in gloomy silence in a room so crowded with Victorian furniture and bric-a-brac that we had to take a deep breath before sitting down at the tea table. Her parents were a very pious couple, and we had to take Grace before and after tea.

On her eleventh birthday, Evangeline begged me to ask her parents' permission to join the Girl Guides. At first they were horrified to think of their frail little girl engaged in such robust activities, but I managed to persuade them at last, on condition that I collect her and return her safely to the fold after every meeting.

I also promised my personal protection. She was so tiny and timid, however, we found her more of a liability than an asset to the Swallow Patrol, but so touchingly grateful for our friendship we hadn't the heart to discourage her. So we dragged her around with us on all our group activities, and Patsy would ride her pig-a-back as we trudged home across the fields.

Rules were strict, and we had an inspection of fingernails at every meeting. Hair must be neat and tidy, belts and badges polished, and hat brims ironed.

"To help other people at all times and to obey the Guide law" was a solemn promise we dared not disobey.

Because I was so cocky and confident, I was chosen to lead the figure-marching at the County Display one year. It was my proudest moment when the Captain struck the opening chords of the "Marche Militaire" and I led the six patrols onto the lawn.

Mother was proud, too, but also a little sad. "I saw your father then," she said.

One of the really important dates in our village calendar was the Flower Show in midsummer. Because it was held in the field opposite our cottage, we always felt a special interest in this exciting event. Hanging out of the bedroom windows, we had a splendid view of all the preparations.

The first to arrive were the Fun Fair Family in Romany caravans, with a trailer piled high with painted wooden sections, which we quickly identified as the roundabout, swings, and sideshows. The black-eyed barefoot children swung open the gate and ran onto the field waving their arms, followed by several thin grey-hounds.

How we envied these wild-looking children who could run barefoot all the time and not only on the beach. The mothers quickly made a campfire, and soon we could smell something savory cooking in a frying pan, and we heard the children called from their play to eat.

They sat on the caravan steps with plates on their knees, and the men had their meal inside.

Then they all began to work hard, erecting the amusements for the following day—men, women, and children all helped, and soon we saw the roundabout with its prancing horses and the hoop-la and firing range all ready. We should have money to spend like other children, and stay up late to swing in the dazzling light of hissing naphthalene flares.

When they were satisfied that everything was ready for their customers, all the men went off to the Rose and Crown, and the women strung out lines of washing and fed their babies on the caravan steps.

The next to arrive were the marquee men—a strong, silent team who wasted no time but heaved and pulled on ropes till the huge tent rose from the ground in a billowy cloud of canvas, and everyone cheered. Then they erected two smaller marquees, one for teas and the other for the judges, and they also went off to the Rose and Crown.

Early the next morning, the gates of the field stood invitingly open, and people began to arrive with trestle tables, tea urns, and wheelbarrows piled with vegetables, great baskets of fruit, and crates of beer and lemonade.

After ten o'clock, we joined the stream of men, women, and children flocking into the big marquee to arrange their exhibits, and got caught up in the fever of excited anticipation. Who had the biggest marrow, the juiciest pears, the finest beans, and the reddest tomatoes? Had Mrs. Smith beaten Mrs. Jones this year with her elderberry wine? And who would win first prize for sausage rolls, and fruit cake, pickles, chutney, marmalade, and jam? (We were secretly relieved when Mother decided not to exhibit her homemade rhubarb jam, for we knew it hadn't jelled.)

Neither could she show any crochet work, knitting, or embroidery, because, unfortunately, Mother was not an expert at any of these accomplishments.

But she once won third prize for her fruit cake, and we were terribly pleased, because we could not bear to see her cake rejected every year in favor of others that were richer or a better shape or the exact shade of brown the judges were looking for. But she always encouraged her children to enter as many classes as possible, and examples of our writing, needlework, and handicrafts all won prizes, also our bunches of wild flowers gathered in fields and woods, riverbanks and marsh, hedgerow and country lane.

One year, we spent weeks before the Flower Show collecting flowers and grasses for William's special exhibit of pressed wild flowers, and Mother lent her heavy flatirons to press out all the juices between sheets of blotting paper, and only got them back just in time to iron our second-best frocks.

But William made a wonderful collection of over one hundred different kinds and gave every one the correct name. We spent hours poring over his nature books and cigarette cards, searching for the Latin names for such local names as "lady's slipper," "milkmaid," and "cuckoo flower" were not allowed. But he won first prize and special praise from the judges, so Mother was very pleased and proud.

All the children of the village with money to spend on this festive day entered the races, to win more money to spend.

They called us the "Sprinting Shears" one year when we all succeeded in winning races in our particular age groups.

The village band, complete with drums, cymbals, and trombone, played loud music in the afternoon and soft music in the evening for dancing.

The Flower Show attracted the whole village, even

the Gentry, who strolled languidly around the marquee, going into ecstasies over the exhibits from their cooks and gardeners—

"I say, old boy, just look at that *fantastic* marrow!"

"Great Scott! Isn't that a superb example of the Delphinium Duchess. How do you do it every year? You clever old thing you!"

"My *dear*, have you seen the marmalade? Isn't it divine!"

Sir Richard Barnaby-Smyth would declare the show open at two-thirty, then retire to the judges' tent for another glass of sherry.

Her Ladyship would distribute prizes at four o'clock, then she, too, would retire to the judges' tent for a special afternoon tea, fanning herself delicately with a lace handkerchief.

Mother was rather reluctant to pay for tea in the marquee, with her own kitchen and kettle just across the road, but when we had taken several prizes and she was pleased with us, we could usually persuade her to stay, and we even paid for her cup of tea and buttered scone.

Henry was growing fast, and he was glowing with health. He had Mother's strong capable hands and her equable temperament—apart from the same tendency to worry about everything and everybody that I had as a young child.

Henry was never idle or lazy, so the word "boredom" had no meaning for him. His busy hands liked to be building or hammering or digging in the small patch of earth where once upon a time Mother had her backyard hens. It was because of Henry and his great longing for a garden that she decided to sell the hens, and one of the neighbors provided several barrow loads of good soil.

Then Henry bought himself a spade. This new interest absorbed all his spare time and surplus energy, and he ran home from school, seized a bucket and shovel, and followed the farm horses down the lane to the blacksmith's shop.

"I must have manure for my garden!" he insisted.

I urged him to plant some flower seeds, but he was not interested in flowers, only vegetables, so I soon lost interest in his garden.

Mother was delighted by this consuming industry in her youngest son and could hardly wait to sample the produce from the first row of lettuces and radishes.

"Would it be possible, Henry, to plant a few potatoes?" she asked tentatively. "And perhaps a row of carrots and parsnips? And, of course, cabbages are always useful."

And Henry, flushed with success, leaned on his spade and measured his small patch of earth with a dubious frown.

"Well, I could grow you a few cabbages here, but the other vegetables I shall grow in my school allotment next year," he decided.

"Thank you, Henry." Mother was satisfied.

Then she took another long look at her youngest son, standing square and sturdy on his first garden, and she said kindly, "You know, Henry, I am a very lucky woman, for I have two sons, and one is clever and one is useful. *I need them both.*" And she gave him one of her rare smiles, so tenderly convincing he had to turn away to hide his tears.

Then he took the man-sized spade and began to dig

with renewed energy till his hands were blistered and his fair head damp with sweat.

We ate Henry's brussels sprouts with our Christmas dinner, and Henry's carrots and parsnips in our stews, but Henry's cabbages went on forever, and I began to wish he would take up fishing for a change.

While Mary wanted everything to remain unchanged forever, in a soft gray pattern of quiet tranquillity, I wanted it colorful and gay. She was shy, hesitant, and gentle still, while I had grown bold and adventurous.

But the little ones were growing up and had their own friends and their own interests, so I hadn't to be constantly anxious about them any more. They preferred the slow motion of one of Henry's "bodgies"—a box on wheels—to the swift passage of the bicycle, and refused to accept my invitation to ride on the carrier.

Now the neighbors said of me, "She's getting exactly like her father." And I could see it was true. Impatient to spread my wings, intolerant of delay, restless, moody, noisy, and bold, Father lived again. But Mother tightened the reins and curbed my restlessness, for she had suffered too much anguish with an erring husband to encourage her daughter in the same tendencies.

"What's the matter with you, child? You used to be such a quiet, contented little girl. Now look at you! Take a good look at yourself, Sarah."

I looked at myself and saw a girl neither pretty nor plain, with a pouting mouth, a freckled nose, searching gray eyes, and two long thick plaits of hair.

I saw a girl in a homemade frock, darned stockings, and patched shoes. And I looked at Mother in doubt and dismay.

"What's wrong with me, then? Tell me what's wrong?"

And I burst into tears and ran out of the house.

Professor Littlejohn was an eccentric old gentleman who owned a row of cottages and collected the rents every Monday morning. With his flowing beard and cultured voice, he looked more like a Jewish rabbi than a landlord. He lived happily and contentedly with three cats in a rambling ivy-covered house with a walled garden, in which he wandered barefoot, even in winter, talking to the birds. Sometimes we would hear him conversing in strange languages to the three cats, and when William left the village school and became a real scholar, he identified the strange languages as Greek and Latin. But no matter what he did or how oddly he behaved, the Professor was always excused because he was eccentric.

This seemed a little unfair to the normal human beings.

We children called him "Professor-do-it-yourself," for he would not employ a laborer for repairs but always did it himself. The results of his labors had to be seen to be believed, for he used a filthy-looking concoction of his own invention—William said it was cow dung mixed with mortar! He would arrive with bucket, trowel, and a light ladder at the most inconvenient time of the day, call out authoritatively, "I shall need your assistance, if you please," and Mother would have to drop everything to stand on the bottom of the ladder with a watchful eye on the bucket perched precariously on the tiles, and knowing its horrible contents.

The same revolting mixture was also used for interior repairs, but, fortunately, it dried on the walls and ceilings as solid as a rock, and Mother hastily covered it with whitewash.

The rent of the cottage (five shillings weekly) was considered fair and reasonable, and Mother was a good tenant and always paid her rent regularly. One of the neighbors, who lacked Mother's strong-mindedness, would sometimes be tempted to buy a new hat with the rent money.

Then the Professor would find a little note pinned on the door when he called, saying, "Sorry, pay next week." He was more than a little vexed.

One of the most useful Jacks-of-all-trades in our village, and a near neighbor of ours, was Benjamin Brown, known simply as "Ben." We depended on Ben for everything, from fixing a broken pram, to taking the collection at church on Sunday.

He was the only son of a widowed mother, and they lived most happily together in a tiny cottage—one of the Professor's—using the front room as a workshop. It was never empty of customers, from seven in the morning till ten at night, for Ben was such a pleasant, comfortable sort of person, and so ready to listen to his customers' troubles, that he sometimes completed the small repairs while they talked and waited.

In summer, the shop door stood invitingly open, and Ben, in shirt sleeves and greasy dungarees, would be working and whistling cheerfully. He was usually surrounded by broken prams, buckled bicycles, and all his useful paraphernalia for unblocking drains and sweeping chimneys.

In winter, the shop was warm and stuffy, with a paraffin stove.

Ben changed his clothes, and his expression, to suit his various roles. Dressed in a black bowler hat, black suit and boots, as a bearer at a funeral, Ben would look as solemn as a judge. As an usher at a wedding, he would grin like a Cheshire cat. Leading his Boy Scout troop on a route march, Ben was earnest and prepared for any emergency. But whether his face was smeared with oil, smudged with soot, or scrubbed clean for a funeral—Ben was Ben!

He was another of William's special friends, and the only reason why he joined the Boy Scouts. Scout law meant nothing to my independent brother, who was a law unto himself, but he was prepared to adopt it, with certain reservations, if Ben was Scoutmaster. When they went to camp at Easter, and the shop was closed for a week, we were completely lost.

Funerals were postponed, drains remained unblocked and chimneys unswept, broken bicycles and prams were tied up with string, and the Vicar had to find a substitute to take the collection on Easter Sunday.

"Ben's back!" The news spread quickly around the village.

The shutters were down, the door stood invitingly open, and Ben, tanned by wind and sun, was whistling a cheery little song of the great outdoors.

He pushed a lock of tow-colored hair out of his eyes, grinned at the queue of impatient customers, and asked, "Well, folks, how's things?" Ben was back!

When we were very young, Mother would only entrust us to the care of one particular neighbor—dear motherly Mrs. Summerfield, a widow with four sons. William and I stayed with her for a week when Mary was born, while Mother was looked after by the Auntie who liked the beach. She also liked babies.

We were told to expect a "nice surprise" on our return home, but William was dismayed and disappointed by the nature of the surprise, for he had expected a toy train.

The next time we stayed with Mrs. Summerfield, we were told vaguely that Mother was taking a few days holiday with Father somewhere in Scotland, where he was on embarkation leave.

The third and last time we took Mary with us, and when we returned home we found Henry.

After that, William flatly refused to stay with Mrs. Summerfield, even for a few hours, because as he explained bluntly to Mother, "We've got enough now!"

Mrs. Summerfield was a plump, comfortable little woman who reminded me of Mrs. Noah. She always had all the time in the world to sit beside the fire or in the open doorway with a child on her lap.

Apart from her four sons, she kept three cats, two dogs, a canary, goldfish, rabbits, and chickens—because her sons liked pets. I believe if they had brought home an elephant, she would have kept it in the back garden. Her sons adored her, and they all were well-mannered good-looking boys, yet they did exactly as they pleased. Their mother spared them any form of discipline or punishment.

Happiness and contentment, so deeply imbued in her, she passed on to her boys, so they stayed at home, were neither clever nor ambitious, courted and married local girls, and, we hope, lived happy ever after.

Because it was such a novelty to have little girls in the house, Mary and I were kissed and cuddled and allowed to feed the pets whenever we pleased.

The boys almost wept when Mother collected us,

for they had hoped to add two small girls to their collection of household pets.

It was a homely little cottage, and the warm welcome we received from this good neighbor and her sons helped to compensate for the loss of Mother.

We all were allowed to do exactly as we pleased and to eat only such food as we really enjoyed: sausages and mash, pork pies, steak and kidney pudding, and homemade quince jam being top favorites. We took no walks, had no fresh air and no exercise other than a walk down the garden to feed the chickens and rabbits. Bedtime was any time at all, when you were ready, and if we fell asleep, as we often did late in the evening on Mrs. Summerfield's lap or Tom's knees, we were carried upstairs, undressed and popped into the middle of a big four-poster bed (warmed by an old-fashioned warming pan). Mary and I, lost in the folds of the soft feather mattress, would wait impatiently for Mrs. Summerfield to join us.

Then, one on either side of her, she gathered us up into her warm, motherly bosom, and we slept till morning.

8

Christmas by Lamplight

Childhood Christmases are divided into two distinct chapters—before and after Father Christmas was explained. The first chapter, in all its trusting simplicity, lasted to the ripe age of seven, when the discovery that it was nothing more than a legend was so shattering that the magic of Christmas vanished abruptly.

It was William who first enlightened me one Christmas Eve when I had gone obediently to bed at six o'clock with Mary and Henry because of the awful possibility of being found awake when Father Christmas called.

Nothing was left for children found awake in their beds—nothing at all!

I could hear William rustling paper in the next room by the light of the candle.

He always left it to the last moment. My own

presents for the family had been tied up for weeks, and were looking a little tatty after much inspection and speculation about their suitability.

There was no mystery or magic about the presents we gave to each other, and they would be found lying on top of the bulging sacks filled by Father Christmas.

I knew the pillowcases were hanging as usual on the brass knobs at the foot of the bed, and they were limp and empty.

I also knew they could be found fat and bulging with presents by five o'clock on Christmas morning. Sometime between the hours of ten—when Mother went to bed—and five—when it was safe to take a peep—this wonderful thing happened.

It was even more wonderful when you consider that Mother reminded us every year not to expect very much, for Father Christmas had first to call on the poor little orphans, the sick children in hospital, and the unfortunate children.

The best and biggest presents were therefore distributed before he ever reached our house, we being the fortunate children with good parents, a good home, and good health. It was the poor unfortunate children that Father Christmas was most concerned about, not us, and so on and so forth.

We listened politely every year, then we hung up our empty pillowcases and climbed into bed with little secret smiles of satisfaction, confident of finding them filled in the morning. I did not want the mystery explained, or the journey of that red-robed white-bearded old gentleman ever to change its colorful conclusion.

The distance from the icy caves of Greenland, where he kept his store of presents for good girls and boys, to our remote village of Kent was covered in the space of a few hours, I considered. The reindeer were faster than horses and had magic in their hoofs, for they did not keep to the roads, but carried the sleigh over the rooftops in a most delightful way. With bells tinkling merrily, and the sleigh piled with parcels, they raced through the night, while the snowflakes drifted down softly and silently like tiny balls of cotton wool onto the red hood and white beard. He always chose the widest chimney in the house, and if you remembered to scamper downstairs quickly on Christmas morning, before Mother lit the fire in the front room, you could see his footprints in the hearth.

A cardboard Father Christmas first appeared in early December over the shop doors of the village stores, supported by two small Christmas trees, garlanded with tinsel and silver stars. Every time Mother went in the shop to buy a pound of this or that, she would remind us of the importance of being good, obedient children, so we supposed he was there for that purpose.

But now I was seven, and too excited to sleep, and William was still wrapping his presents for Mother and Mary, Henry and me. I wondered whether I should get another pencil and rubber. I had received a pencil and rubber from William every year since I was four, and he couldn't seem to think of anything else to buy. William was like that.

Mother said it was because he was not very imaginative, but anyway a pencil and rubber was always useful because I did a lot of writing and rubbing out. He might give me a pencil sharpener as well, then I should not have to bother him any more to sharpen my pencils with his penknife. But they didn't understand,

and I didn't want useful presents for Christmas, only books and lovely, surprising useless things.

William was rustling paper as I crept out of bed to warn him of the awful possibility of being left without presents, supposing he was still awake when Father Christmas called.

It was a wonderful night, and a million stars twinkled in the sky. Away in the distance, I could hear the sleigh bells, so I hurried into William's room.

He was sitting in the middle of the bed, surrounded by paper and bits of string. A large bulky parcel was wedged between his knees, and he looked rather cross when I trailed in.

"Go away!" he ordered, scowling at me in the candlelight.

I explained as quickly as I could about Father Christmas.

"Then why aren't you asleep?" he demanded.

That was the sort of question I expected from William, so I explained again that I was going to sleep the instant I got back to bed, but I was worried about him. Had he nearly finished?

No he hadn't, and anyway there was no hurry, for it was all a lot of silly twaddle, and I was a baby to believe in it still. What did he mean? He was hugging his knees, and his eyes were dark and secretive.

"If I tell you, you must promise faithfully not to tell Mary—promise?"

I nodded, shivering with cold, fear, and excitement.

"Cross your heart and hope to die?"

I crossed my heart and hoped to die, if I told Mary —what?

"There isn't a real Father Christmas. It's just a

fairy story. Mother fills the pillowcases," he told me importantly.

I stared back at him, speechless with shock.

"It's true," he said with cruel insistence. I didn't want to believe it, but I had to believe it, for William did not lie.

Next to Mother, he was the most honest, the most truthful, and the bravest person in the world.

"I knew about it ages ago," he explained, "but Mother made me promise not to tell you till you were seven. It's just for little children, see? Now me and you have to keep it a secret from Mary and Henry."

It softened the blow a little, to be big enough to share this important secret with William, but I was still shivering and shaking and wishing he hadn't told me. I wanted to know where Mother got all the presents to fill the pillowcases.

"Oh, from Grandmother and the Aunties and the neighbors and all over the place, silly!" he told me. "Now, you just pretend to be asleep and when Mother comes to bed, you'll see! Now go away, I want to finish this."

He gave me a push, and I left him, whimpering, "Now you've s-s-spoilt everything!"

Snowflakes were falling softly on the rooftops now. I listened carefully, but there was no sound of sleigh bells in the distance. So I crept back to bed and curled my icy feet in my long flannelette nightgown and lay still—waiting for Mother.

The church clock struck every quarter of an hour, and I had to recite to myself to keep awake—Sunday School texts and familiar hymns, "Now the Day Is Over" and "There Is a Green Hill Far Away," and then our favorite carol, "Away in a Manger."

Mary lay snug and warm beside me, still wrapped in the mystery and magic of Christmas Eve, still young enough to be spared this shattering discovery.

Then, at last, I heard a movement on the stairs, and the door opened slowly and cautiously—a hand slid along the bedrail, and a foot creaked on a loose floorboard. Under the bedclothes I could hear my heart thudding, and I wanted to sneeze.

A moment later, the candlelight in the next room flickered on the wall and disappeared.

It was safe now to sit up and feel for the empty pillowcase. It had gone!

I crept back under the clothes, licking the salty tears with the tip of my tongue as they rolled slowly down the side of my nose.

Once more the church clock struck another quarter-hour in the silent night; once more the stairs creaked with stealthy footsteps, and the candlelight flickered in the next room, and a hand crept cautiously along the bedrail. A heavy object dropped from the brass knob at my end of the bed, and another at Mary's end. Back and forth went the stealthy footsteps carefully over the loose floorboards.

Then all is finished. It is dark and quiet. Mary stirs in her sleep, and I put my arm around her.

With a little sob, my wet face brushes her hair. "It's all spoilt," I whimper as I fall asleep.

"Father Christmas has been very generous this year," said Mother brightly as we emptied our pillowcases on her bed at six o'clock the following morning.

William exchanged a secret smile with me and agreed with Mother that he was jolly good and I hadn't expected to see so many presents. Now I knew why two of my favorite books, *Andersen's Fairy Tales* and *Uncle Tom's Cabin*, were included this year, as well as a new skipping rope, some doll's furniture, a peg top, and some colored marbles—all things I wanted badly.

And something new to wear—gloves, stockings, and nightgowns—that pleased Mother more than me.

Right at the bottom, when we thought we had finished, we found a pink sugar mouse and a sixpence.

The church bells were ringing a Christmas carol, and Mother's face in the lamplight was the face of Mary, the Mother of Jesus. She sat in the middle of her big bed, with Mary on one side and Henry on the other, and William was tucked in the bottom with me.

We smiled happily across the mountain of paper, toys, and games scattered over the bed.

And again Mother reminded us what fortunate children we were, and of the kindness of Father Christmas.

Dear Mother! I crawled over the mountain of paper to give her a hug.

"Thank you! Oh, thank you!"

Then I whispered in her ear that I knew she had filled the pillowcases, and I promised not to tell the little ones.

William looked a little guilty at the bottom of the bed as she shook her head reprovingly. Then she took my face in her hands and kissed me with a warm tenderness.

"Then you must write your own thank-you letters this year!" she whispered, her eyes mischievous as a child's as she unwrapped a spinning top for Henry.

The kitchen and the front room were draped with our homemade paper chains. We had sat around the kitchen table, with a bowl of flour paste and packets of colored strips of paper costing one halfpenny a packet, for several of our Children's Hours the week before Christmas.

The chains were sticky with paste when we had finished, and Henry, who insisted on helping, had twisted the loops into queer shapes, but Mother draped them across the whitewashed ceilings and said they looked very pretty.

A small Christmas tree, festooned with tinsel and sugar mice, stood in an old enamel bucket on the corner table, and Mother had draped the bucket in red crinkled paper to hide its ugliness.

She left us on the bed, playing with our presents, and went downstairs to put another log on the fire and make a pot of tea.

Then she started to fry the sausages for breakfast—we usually had porridge or Grape-nuts—so when the appetizing smell drifted up to the bedroom, we all trailed down, wearing thick jerseys. (Dressing gowns were considered a luxury we could not afford.)

We left behind us a litter of paper and string and empty boxes and four empty crumpled pillowcases and a pink sugar mouse someone had dropped on the stairs.

We children did most of our Christmas shopping at Miss Baker's haberdashery in the village.

She began to prepare her Christmas window at the end of November by clearing out all the haberdashery and replacing it with toys, games, and books.

We watched the transformation every day on our way to and from school and encouraged Miss Baker to greater efforts by our praise and appreciation. She fussed and flustered in and out of the window, and every few minutes would dart outside to see the customer's view from the pavement. She started by covering the floor and shelves with red and green paper, then she popped outside, asked our opinion on the color scheme, and decided to have a little frill around it. The floor was then completely covered with a selection of small toys, humming tops, skipping ropes, boxes of paints, and colored pencils.

Then she built up a wonderful display on the shelves on either side of the window—Snakes and Ladders, Ludo, Snap, and Happy Families; jigsaw puzzles, fretwork, and tool sets for the boys; and wool and embroidery sets for the girls. Larger and more expensive toys were always arranged on a shelf in the center of the window to attract the few customers who could afford to pay the price. We admired them, but could not afford to buy them. Books were displayed on another shelf, and dolls stood gracefully in between.

Miss Baker always started off with this neat and careful arrangement, spending a whole week on the display, but it didn't stay that way, for as soon as she had finished her Christmas window, the customers began to push into the shop, eager to turn it all out again.

Poor Miss Baker, bullied by her customers—who all insisted on something from the window—was more flustered than ever, and soon the window was a glorious jumble of toys, games, books, dolls, humming tops, peg tops, and little string bags of colored marbles.

We liked it this way, and it was more fun than her original plan for Christmas.

Little ones had to be lifted up to hang on the window ledge, and we had to breathe our hot breath on the frosted glass and wipe the window with our scarves and muffs to see in properly.

With the front window all ready for "the dear children," Miss Baker turned her attention to the small side window, and here we had to climb on the fence to see in properly.

In this window, we selected our presents for Mother, Grandmother, and the Aunties. After much careful deliberation, we usually decided to buy handkerchiefs (price a penny and three farthings each), for the splendid selection allowed for a different pattern or color for each recipient. Grandmother always had white linen, the Aunties had stripes, and Mother's was patterned with roses or violets. William and the little ones were perfectly satisfied with their choice of handkerchiefs, but I was never quite satisfied and searched frantically for a "novelty" at a price I could afford. This made me rather unpopular when we did our Christmas shopping, and William would go off in a huff, leaving me still undecided at the shop window, clutching my precious savings in a purse.

I found it a most worrying business as a small girl, and although I made a careful list of people and a list of "suggestions"—this was Mother's idea—it didn't work out that way.

Apart from the family, we also bought Christmas presents for our best friends to be exchanged the last day of term, and halfpenny Christmas cards for our second-best friends, teachers, and neighbors—these were delivered by hand to save postage.

Mother always headed the list, and once I was tempted to spend the enormous sum of three and elevenpence three farthings on a most elaborate pink satin nightdress case in a pretty box.

This left me with exactly one and elevenpence halfpenny to spend on all the rest. I quickly realized I had made a sad mistake, but it was too late, and I was too proud to ask Miss Baker to take it back. My head ached with the effort of working out the remainder to the best advantage.

That was the year the Aunties had to share a small box of licorice allsorts between them, and my secondbest friends and the teachers and neighbors all had homemade Christmas cards. Since I had no talent whatsoever in painting or drawing, my shepherds and sheep under a starry sky were mistaken for a gypsy encampment, and the Baby Jesus was obviously Mary's doll!

But then I decided all the worry and effort had not been wasted, after all, for Mother's amazement on Christmas morning gave me such a lovely feeling of self-importance.

It pleased my vanity to see this beautiful expensive present shown with pride to the neighbors, and then to see it put carefully away, wrapped in tissue paper in Mother's drawer.

It was "too good" to use every day, she said, and would only be used on very special and important occasions that would include her birthday and the next visit of Grandmother and possibly Easter Sunday.

So I was satisfied that my precious savings had not been wasted.

After Father Christmas had been carefully "explained" by Mother, and the shock of William's blunt announcement had been soothed by a sack of presents, I felt I could bear to face the cruel facts of life more calmly.

Although the mystery and magic of Christmas had gone forever, I still had the Baby Jesus—and it was still His birthday.

I was deeply religious at this period and determined on being a missionary in Darkest Africa.

"Search the Scriptures" was my new motto, and it hung over my bed in gilt lettering.

Bible stories once again took priority over fairy stories, and I learned a lot of texts and passages from the Psalms.

The Band of Hope attracted me like a magnet, and their rousing choruses I practiced so thoroughly even Mother began to wish I would adopt a secular pastime. Sunday School and chapel, morning and evening, kept me busy on Sundays, and even the afternoon walk in our Sunday best clothes lost its attraction, for it seemed such a shocking waste of time.

"Gosh! She's nuts!" William declared scornfully when I explained the reason for such intense religious activity. "A missionary? You would run a mile if you saw a snake! Didn't you know they had snakes in Africa, silly?" No, I hadn't known about the snakes.

Lions and tigers and even crocodiles I felt could be dealt with, in their proper perspective, of course, but snakes?

"Never mind, Sarah, you can be a Sunday School teacher instead," said Mother soothingly.

She was not at all surprised, therefore, when I taught Mary to sing "Away in a Manger" that Christmas, and we both trailed down in our nightgowns for the first performance, while the sausages frizzled a nice crispy brown.

Henry joined in from under the kitchen table, where he was building a castle of bricks, and spoiled the harmony, but Mother said it sounded very nice and we could sing it again later.

With a blazing log fire in the front room all day; with Snap, Happy Families, Snakes and Ladders, and Ludo; with Henry's new humming top and Mary's new doll; with sausages for breakfast and roast beef and Christmas pudding for dinner; with crackers to pull, chestnuts to roast, and sugar mice to eat—it was a wonderfully happy day.

Mother left the Christmas pudding in a black iron saucepan on top of the kitchen stove and the beef in the oven, then we all started out for chapel to sing more carols.

We all had helped to make the Christmas pudding —stoning raisins, chopping suet, washing currants, beating eggs, and mixing. Everyone must stir and make a wish, Mother insisted, even Henry, who didn't understand about the wish and thought he had to eat it in its raw state! We knew that Mother had saved a few silver threepenny bits and they were hidden in the pudding.

We wore our new gloves and scarves, and Mary and I carried new muffs—a present from Grandmother.

Everyone called, "Happy Christmas!" and we called back.

The fields and hedges were draped in blankets of snow, and the bells were ringing a merry peal. We met the whole village on the way to church or chapel. The postman was delivering his last load of parcels and cards, and the milkman clattering his can on the icy doorsteps and filling up milk jugs. The Gentry, who had big house parties at Christmas and New Year, brought their guests to church in carriages or in one of the new-fangled petrol-driven automobiles that made all the dogs bark and all the mothers gather their small children under their skirts for protection. Some of the young gentlemen rode their horses to church and left them in charge of a groom.

"Your father would enjoy this lovely Christmas pudding," Mother would say every year as she stuck a sprig of holly in the top—we never had Father for Christmas.

"I hope your father has received his presents and cards safely," she mused in the late afternoon.

Since we had to post them at the end of the hop-picking season, we had forgotten all about them.

"You must write and thank your father, William, for the money he sent to buy toys and books," she reminded him as we drank hot cocoa in the firelight.

Now I was seven, and Father Christmas had been nicely explained, so I had also to write some thank-you letters.

I had received a box of children's stationery containing six blue and six pink tiny sheets of notepaper with matching envelopes. I started on the thank-you letters right away, for it was such a novelty. The letters were written in bold style, short but adequate. They read as follows:

"Thank you very much for your lovely present. I hope you are well. With love and kisses from Sarah."

William suggested that his name could be included in the letter—love from William and Sarah, but Mother was adamant, and he finally finished his thank-you letters a month or so later.

After Father Christmas was explained, I began to make my own gifts for the family, with a little help from Mother, so the following Christmas Mary received a doll's cradle, fashioned from a shoe box, with lace curtains.

Henry took a poor view of the black golliwog, though—a stocking stuffed with rags, with white buttons for eyes, nose, and mouth, and a red waistcoat made from an old tea cozy.

"What's this?" he demanded, holding it upside down.

"It's a g-g-golliwog, and I m-m-made it all by m-m-myself!" I told him proudly.

He gave me a withering look.

The following year, I upset William, and he was very cool towards me for the rest of the day.

He didn't want a shoe bag. He wanted a catapult.

So we played our last games of Snap and Happy Families, and Mary and I sang "Away in a Manger" for the third time. ("Gosh! not again?" muttered William.) So ended our Christmas by lamplight.

When Mother took a lodger, she changed the pattern of Christmas morning to include him.

We no longer emptied our sacks on her bed, but trailed them downstairs to the front room to sit on the floor, with a blazing log fire in the hearth, and the lodger in pajamas and dressing gown yawning and stretching in the big armchair. Mother was a little worried and fussed after we had awakened him and dragged him out of bed.

Perhaps a lodger would prefer not to be disturbed at six o'clock on Christmas morning?

But he assured her he wouldn't have missed it for the world, and it was wonderful to have a family at Christmastime.

We children bought him a rather flashy tie pin the first Christmas, and he bought us a marvelous combined present that was a complete surprise—not even Mother knew about it, for he had hidden it in his bedroom on Christmas Eve. It was a pedal scooter with rubber-tired wheels, and the latest model on the market. We thanked him so profusely he was quite embarrassed.

Apart from the presents we had from Father when he came home from Mesopotamia after the war, that scooter was the only expensive toy we had in the whole of our childhood.

Now we had a lodger to help us make the paper chains, mix the pudding, and advise us on buying presents for the family. We consulted him on everything. Now we had roast chicken for dinner on Christmas Day instead of roast beef!

9

Aniseed Balls and Humbugs

The hop-picking season, starting in mid-August and lasting till late September, was another episode of our childhood in Kent.

It roused the sleepy village to a feverish activity in the drowsy days of late summer when a golden haze hung over the stubble fields, where hay and barley, wheat and oats had already been harvested.

The green arches of the hop gardens, stretching across the furrowed earth down in the valley in long, straight avenues, were strung with hops like grapes in a vast conservatory.

The kilns were fired in the oast houses, the apples and pears picked and ready for sale to the hop pickers in all the farmhouse sculleries—at threepence a pound. The farmers and their bailiffs were making the last rounds of their fertile acres, with dogs at their heels, checking on the huts and sanitation arrangements for their pickers; the hop bins were ready stacked in the barns, and the heavy wagons ready in the yards.

Back in the village, the shopkeepers took their rolls of wire netting out of store and nailed it up to their counters, making themselves a barricade against the horde of invaders.

There would be gypsies in Romany caravans, strange wild-looking people with barefoot children, and "foreigners" from the Mile End Road or the Elephant and Castle.

The shopkeepers didn't trust any of them. Everything was put away out of reach and temptation, and nothing remained on the counters save this ugly barricade of wire.

Poor Miss Baker, flushed and flustered and tormented with doubt, gathered up her haberdashery and hid it away under the counter. Then she disinfected the shop with Jeyes Fluid, and put up a notice that read, NO CREDIT ALLOWED.

For the benefit of those ignorant strangers who would ask, "What's credit?" she added, CASH CUSTOMERS ONLY.

The grocer also believed in the good properties of Jeyes Fluid, and instructed the grocer's boy to sprinkle it liberally over the shop floor several times a day. He also took the precaution to cover his bacon, butter, cheese, and sausages with muslin, for who could tell what horrible germs were lurking in the clothes of those scruffy-looking cockneys?

He was quite sure they never took a bath, and their language was appalling. As for the gypsies, well, they were just a lot of no good scallywags, with thieving children!

The grocer was taking no chances. He was a good

God-fearing man, but there was a hint to a man's discipleship. Neither cockneys nor gypsies could be included in the category of neighbor, and to love them, as commanded in the Gospels, was asking too much.

So behind his barricade of wire, he was ready for battle when the first hop-picking contingent arrived.

The butcher had a barrel of clean sawdust delivered from the timber yard, and the butcher's boy had been instructed to "chuck it about in great handfuls" on the floor.

He also instructed his wife and daughter to keep out of sight, for gypsy men were notoriously greedy for women, and carefully camouflaged his cash desk with posters of New Zealand mutton.

The Vicar took the precaution of removing all the charity boxes, then he, too, put up a notice on the church door: ALL ARE WELCOME.

At the Rose and Crown, extra staff were engaged to serve the thirsty customers, outside the premises.

Long trestle tables and benches were brought up from the cellar and placed in convenient positions on the forecourt and the back yard, and drays arrived from the breweries with crates of beer, cider, and Guinness. The landlord, in his shirt sleeves, and the bartenders, sweating and swearing like troopers, worked far into the night preparing their premises for the onslaught. Plentiful supplies of pork pies had been ordered, and bottles of pop and potato crisps for the hop pickers' children, who apparently lived on the stuff.

Sometimes the small fry would demand fish and chips but their mums would clamp down on them smartly with a good sound box around the ears, and young Alfie or Maudie had to make do with pop and crisps.

180

"Nah don't you start any of your nonsense dahn 'ere, or I'll send yer back 'ome!" was sufficient to quell any rebellion among the small fry. It was a threat that never failed to restore order, and a proper respect for their elders.

So the publican and his wife were ready for business. "Customers is customers," they decided sensibly.

To the children of the slums of east and southeast London, this annual exodus to the hop fields was a glimpse of Eden—but they tired of Eden and, like Adam and Eve, were glad to evacuate with their forbidden fruit.

It was, however, the only kind of holiday they expected or experienced fifty years ago, and, although they were supposed to pick hops from seven in the morning till five in the evening, they managed to escape into the surrounding woods a dozen times a day.

Irate mothers would yell, "Alfie!" "Maudie!" "Frankie!" "Katie!" and threaten the most awful punishment if they didn't return to work, but the woods echoed with their cheeky cockney voices, their rough play, and the latest songs from the London music halls.

They wore their oldest clothes, which soon became as ragged as the gypsies', and they copied the gypsies and ran barefoot into the woods. But the cockney children and the gypsy children did not mix, they were too suspicious of each other.

The gypsies seemed a little afraid of the others, who swarmed in crowds over their familiar landscape, and they stood shyly around in small groups biting their nails.

"Dirty gypsies! Lousy gypsies!" jeered the London children, and tormented them with hazel sticks and squashed blackberries.

They were alien in their ways and in their language and had nothing to say to each other that was kind or understanding.

But the gypsy children were more obedient and more disciplined in spite of their wild appearance, and they had to work much harder, for they had their fathers and elder brothers with them in the hop fields, whose hands dealt heavy blows to playful or idle children. We often saw them in tears.

The London children saw their fathers and big brothers only on Sundays, when special excursion trains brought them down for the day, but during the war they did not see them at all, for the excursions were stopped.

The cockney mothers, we noticed, with threats of awful punishment, and even murder, often did nothing more than push their cheeky, rebellious children back to the bins when they finally came back to work.

Sometimes an irate mother would give chase over the plowed field in cheap high-heeled shoes that would crack and bend and drop off in a furrow.

"Blimey! She's 'ad it!" the others would scream. Mothers and children would shriek with laughter and pelt one another with hops, while the poor unfortunate woman would limp painfully back in her stockinged feet.

Everything they did, everything they said was excessively noisy, funny, and rude. They appeared to have no permanent standards of behavior for their children, and could be cruel or kind, strict or indulgent, all in the space of few moments. And they had no fear of anything —save a solitary country lane, and a cow that suddenly mooed over the hedge. Mother told us they missed the noisy traffic of the London streets, the barrow boys, the fish and chip shops, and the cheerful gossip of neighbors on the doorstep.

They were happiest in crowds, so many of the women brought their own children and the neighbor's children, too, and they crowded into the tiny huts provided on the farms, with children and grandparents, dogs, cats, and canaries, pots and pans and bundles of bedding. Some brought concertinas and others brought gramophones with big horns and lots of rather scratchy records to make a good noise.

A small cook house under a drafty hedge or a campfire in the open, according to the weather, were the only means of cooking a meal, so they lived on sausages, fried eggs, and stews.

"Coo, ain't it lovely 'ere, mister?"

The children crowded excitedly around the back door of the farmhouse in a friendly bunch.

"Got any napples? Crikey! Threepence a pahnd? Get 'em for twopence on the barrer."

"Say, mister, got any firewood? Ma says she'll give me a good clip round the ear-ole if I don't find no faggots."

"Mister! 'ere, mister! Got somefink for nofink? Garn! be a sport! I'm picking the 'ops, ain't I?"

"Say, mister, Ma wants a cabbage, a big 'un, an' she don't want no mud on it, see. Twopence? Caw, you're kidding."

"Damage, mister? Gates left open and cattle straying? Broken fences and stolen apples? Whatcher take us for then—a bunch o' nooligans?"

And they march away with an injured air to tell their mums. Oh, but they're crafty and cunning as little foxes, these children from the Mile End Road and the

Elephant and Castle, and we seem, in comparison, slow-witted country bumpkins.

Imagine, for instance, being clever enough to make yourself so objectionable picking the hops into the bin that your mother in desperation would shout, " 'Op it! Go on, 'op it!" and chase you away with a hop bin.

It was inconceivable.

Imagine also being clever enough to make yourself sick on blackberries, and to come back groaning with pain and holding your stomach, from the woods where you had spent the past two hours. So instead of being murdered, you were cosseted and comforted and spent the rest of the day lying comfortably wrapped in grand-mother's shawl? It was inconceivable.

Because we were picking hops like gypsies and cockneys was no excuse for slacking, bad manners, or rudeness, Mother contended. Besides, we picked with the rather exclusive "home pickers" set that included the farmer's wife and daughters. It gave us a certain class distinction that we hadn't to mix with the others. Mother still looked extremely genteel, even perched un-comfortably on the side of a hop bin, for she wore her second-best straw hat, a clean striped blouse, and a wide skirt.

She polished her muddy boots and ours every evening.

We hated picking hops, and every year we hoped (and I prayed) for a miracle in early August so that we needn't start on this dirty, tedious, unrewarding work—unrewarding save for a Saturday sixpence.

Perhaps a long-lost uncle in Australia would die and leave us a fortune? Or father's irresponsible ghost would suddenly turn into one of those sensible, reliable husbands who always provided their wives with a regular income? But nothing ever happened, and once again my passionate pleas to the Almighty went unanswered, and Mother reminded us that the holidays were over—after only two weeks—and the remaining six weeks were provided by the education authorities solely for hop-picking. We needed the money to buy our winter boots and coats, she explained.

There was no escape. Her decision was final. Her word was law. Sulkily and sleepily, we were shepherded from our beds to the kitchen at precisely five-forty-five A.M. to eat a bowl of porridge, while Mother packed the well of the pram with food to last the day—sandwiches, homemade cake, cold bread pudding, and two flasks of tea.

All the neighbors went hop-picking to different farms and pushed their babies and younger children in iron-wheeled carts with strong hoods. But Mother was too proud, so she struggled with the big pram across the plowed fields and muddy cart tracks, and we had to help her, one pushing and one pulling.

But the farm she had selected for our patronage was three miles away, and we had to walk there, and back in the evening. By starting out at six o'clock and walking briskly, we just managed to arrive at the field gate when the farm bailiff called, "All to work!" at seven o'clock. But only the home pickers arrived virtuously at seven o'clock to set a good example to the rest—who were not even aware of our early arrival. William pointed this out frequently to Mother, but she insisted that we continue with this early start because of the principle of the thing and because the farmer had told her the picking started at seven o'clock and finished at five o'clock with an hour for dinner, and on Saturdays from seven o'clock till noon. We must be punctual, she explained, for punctuality would be required of us later in life.

Half an hour later, the gypsies trailed out of their caravans in the next field and approached their separate set of bins with sly and stealthy movements, dragging their whimpering children by the hand. From eight o'clock onwards, the cockneys arrived, yawning and grumbling about the early start, the farmer, the weather, and the hops. They were not at their best in the early morning, and their children were cross and sulky because they, too, had been dragged out of bed and driven out to the hop fields without breakfast. Babies yelled in protest as they jolted over huge clods of earth in their frail little pushcarts, the wheels buckling under them.

It was bedlam when the cockneys arrived, and the mothers' shrill voices echoed down the green arches. But any diversion was better than picking hops! Soon we began to fidget and asked to be "excused." Mother sighed as she repeated her careful instructions, and we ran off into the woods—to hunt for hazelnuts and blackberries and to watch the little red squirrels chasing each other up and down the branches.

When we came back some time later, we asked for a slice of cake because we were hungry, and William emptied the water bottle and had to go back to the farm to refill it for the little ones. Mother offered us tea from the flask—to save time, for time was precious, and we were wasting it. But we stubbornly refused to drink anything but water—lovely ice-cold water from the spring.

We sipped it slowly to aggravate Mother still more.

"When I grow up, *my* children will never have to p-p-pick hops!" I told her scathingly.

If the weather was fine, we stepped out bravely

and Mother was pleased with us, but often we would leave home in a shower, muffled in sou'westers and mackintoshes, grumbling about the discomfort, the long walk, and the way we had to work in the holidays. Then Mother would get cross and remind us of our duty and the dire necessity of those winter boots.

When the mists of early autumn hung over the valley, the hopbines would be drenched, and all the children reluctant to start picking wet hops.

Then Mother would tempt us with a choice of picking either into an upturned umbrella or into a small section of her bin, divided from her part with a length of twine. Despairing of our full co-operation, she would even bribe us with chocolate!

The hops had been sprayed with sulphur, and the sulphur stained our hands with a horrid greenish-black stain that could only be removed with pumice stone and scrubbing brush.

A dozen times a day, I held out my hands for inspection, wailing, "Look! Look! I'm s-s-stained!"

I was much too fastidious, said Mother, and anyway it proved I was working.

Although I always insisted on a clean white handkerchief to wrap around my sandwiches and cake, I still could taste the bitterness of sulphur.

When we were very young, too young to pick hops, we often spent the whole afternoon lying asleep on Mother's coat, spread over a pile of stripped hopbines. The weather was so variable during the hop-picking season, however, that we could be sitting under the umbrella sheltering from the burning sun one day, and the next day sitting under the same umbrella sheltering from a rainstorm. Some days the dust rose in clouds from the wheels of the wagon as it trundled away with a load of hops to the oast house—and other days we wallowed in mud.

Mother would work diligently, hour after hour, stopping only to give us food or to persuade the little ones to take another nap.

At noon, the bailiff's voice would shout, "All to dinner!" and again on the stroke of one, "All to work!"

We never missed the first call, but the second call we ignored completely, though it echoed through the woods and shouted from the treetops: "All to work! All to work!"

Not a child was in sight, save the babies on their mothers' laps; the golden silence of midday hung over the hop fields. It would seem that a Pied Piper had spirited the children away, for the cockneys, the gypsies, and the home children had all disappeared.

Mothers would listen carefully for the sound of a child's voice or a boy's whistle. Half an hour passed, and still the children were missing.

Then the shouting would start again: "Alfie!" "Maudie!" "Frankie!" "Katie!" Once again the little cockneys were threatened with the most awful punishment. "I'll *beat* you, Alfie!" "Just wait till I get my 'ands on you, my girl!" "I'll shake the daylights out of young Katie!"

The gypsy mothers did not shout, but the fathers stalked away angrily and dragged the children back in tears.

When William was eleven and I was nine, Mother had to think of a new way to bribe us to pick more hops. So she asked for a bin with two separate halves, and for two separate books in which the number of bushels could be entered morning and afternoon.

We were terribly proud of the book, for it had our two names on the cover. The measurer always took smaller bushels from our side of the bin than from Mother's side.

We sat on either side of the bin, balanced uncomfortably on the wooden framework, and scooped off the hops with nimble fingers. Then I got careless and scooped off leaves as well, and William made me hang upside down in the bin to clear them out, before the measurer came!

Mother was delighted with this new experiment and promised us each ten shillings to spend in Tunbridge Wells at the end of the hop-picking season.

"Ten shillings!" gasped William. "Gosh! Thanks!" and he tore off the hops with frantic enthusiasm.

Gradually the novelty faded, however, and we slipped back into careless ways, taking turns to be "excused" and to run away into the woods.

We spent a lot of time collecting water and apples from the farm, in taking Henry to see the horses and Mary to see the gypsy babies.

Then Mother despaired of ever getting enough money for all our winter boots and coats. She would work out the price in her head, then check the number of bushels we had picked to date. Sometimes we picked five or six bushels of hops to earn a shilling.

Then the cockneys went on strike and refused to pick another hop till the farmer raised the rate to four bushels for a shilling. This was great fun, for we children played for several hours while the dispute was settled. The home pickers were not allowed to strike, but had to accept the rate agreed upon by the others.

The green hop garden, strung with a framework of poles and wires, was left as stripped and bare as the fields of stubble that surrounded it; the bins were standing at the edge of the field waiting to be moved on to the next hop garden further down the lane. The naked field we left behind was grim and ugly, with its untidy heaps of stripped bines, the trodden earth, and the litter of paper bags, empty cartons, chocolate wrappings, and bottles the children had tossed away. Lying in the furrows at regular intervals were the solid little squares of cold bread pudding I myself had tossed away! I loathed the cold bread pudding, but sometimes I was so hungry I had to accept a piece in the late afternoon when all the sandwiches and cake had been eaten. Then I took a cautious nibble, shuddered with distaste, and dropped it in the nearest furrow when Mother turned her head away.

We all seemed ravenously hungry, out in the open air from dawn till dusk, and we acquired healthy tans. Soon we were looking like gypsies ourselves, and the three separate sets of children, segregated by alien ways of life and behavior, so closely resembled each other after several weeks in the hop fields, the mothers would wonder which was which.

We envied the gypsies because they ran barefoot all the time, and had lovely savory food cooked over a campfire, while we ate sandwiches and cold bread pudding.

We envied the cockneys their noisy, crowded lives.

But nobody envied us.

"Crikey! them kids is proper soppy!" we heard them say as we dutifully followed Mother.

Then William would scowl rebelliously and threaten to go on strike, and I would pout and sulk—just to prove we were not soppy.

When the bines were wet with morning mist or a

190

shower of rain, we refused to pick till they were shaken dry, and when they were scorched by the sun, we complained of scratches. Poor Mother! She wilted in the sun, but enjoyed the morning mist and was not dismayed by a heavy shower.

"It will pass," she would say complacently, still picking hops, while I crouched under the large umbrella with William, and Mary was popped under the hood with young Henry. We were proud of her then, for she sat so erect and dignified on the edge of the bin— she might have been her Ladyship from Cowley Manor, sitting her hunter side-saddle! Mother never complained of tiredness or grumbled about the weather or the hops, but went gallantly on for six long weeks, determined to reach the target she had set herself. She measured each bushel of hops in terms of pence, and could already foresee the satisfying moment when her four children in stockinged feet at Freeman, Hardy, and Willis awaited their turn to be fitted with a pair of new boots!

But the days were long, the work was hard, and her children tiresome and reluctant to pick the hops. Her busy day started at five in the morning and finished at ten in the evening. The long trek home, pushing the heavy pram, often with her two youngest children dropping off to sleep inside and the others dragging on the handle, nearly defeated her, but not quite.

Sinking thankfully into a kitchen chair, she would wait for the kettle to boil, make a pot of tea, and sip it slowly—her body drooping with fatigue.

"There's nothing in this world so refreshing as a nice cup of tea," she would say.

"I want a cup of tea!" we chorused, kicking off our muddy boots.

Then she would pour us each a cup of sweet hot tea, and we stood around the kitchen table watching her, relaxed in her chair "just for ten minutes to recuperate."

"How many more days? How much longer?" William would ask, and Mother would smile bravely.

"Only a few more days, if we *all* work hard."

But already I was demanding hot water and pumice stone to get rid of the horrid stain on my hands, and the little ones had to be washed and undressed ready for bed.

Then we all sat down to a high tea and by seven o'clock we were in bed, and Mother ready to start on her evening chores, for she had time only to make the beds in the morning. Five pairs of boots had to be washed clean of mud, dried on the stove, then polished with Cherry Blossom boot polish. There were dirty clothes to be washed, cakes to bake, bacon to boil, and sandwiches to cut ready for the morrow.

Then she tidied the kitchen, laid breakfast, and made herself a final cup of tea. Exhausted but satisfied, she climbed the stairs, peeped at her four healthy sleeping children, undressed by candlelight, and sank gratefully into the soft folds of the feather bed.

Saturday morning held a nice feeling of anticipation as we stepped out for the hop fields on the stroke of six o'clock, for at noon the farm bailiff would call in sonorous tones, "No more bines to be pulled today!"

Then we children cheered and clapped our hands and rushed Mother away from the hops with all speed. We ran on ahead, eager to drag off our muddy boots and old clothes, to wash away the smell of hops, and receive our sixpence reward for the week's work.

Mrs. Mercer's sweetshop was crowded on Saturday afternoons in the hop-picking season, and we had to wait our turn in the long queue of children. The cockneys and the gypsies all swarmed to the village to do their shopping and enjoy the evening at the Rose and Crown. All the children had money to spend. Dear old Mrs. Mercer had reluctantly agreed to the general plan of barricading the counter against the invaders, but her wire netting was only moderately high, and small hands could still reach up and point to their choice of sweets on the counter.

Aniseed balls and humbugs were the firm favorites with the young cockneys, so Mrs. Mercer ordered a large supply for them. She did not mind these cheeky noisy customers and called them her "little London sparrows."

"And what would you like, my dear?" she would ask politely.

"Aniseed balls and 'umbugs!" came the prompt reply.

"Twelve a penny? Blimey! Twenty a penny on the barrer back 'ome?"

"Is that so, my dear?" The shrewd old eyes twinkled. "Well, in that case, perhaps you would rather not?"

"Garn! 'e's only kiddin'!" they chorused, pushing their way to the counter to get a better view of the varied assortment.

Some of the older girls were more selective and took ages to make up their minds, asking "'Ow much?" or "'Ave you got anything else?" when the counter was already crammed with boxes and the shelves with jars.

But the old lady never wearied or grew impatient, for she considered all her customers had the right to take as much time as they pleased over their choice of sweets.

The boys would tumble out of the shop and drag the little ones onto the churchyard wall, where they sat munching and chewing and sticking out their tongues at the village children, still waiting their turn to be served. Then one of the boys would smash his humbugs in a thousand pieces, against the wall, and a wail of dismay followed the broken fragments. Scrambling on hands and knees in the road, they gathered them up and stuffed their mouths full.

We gazed in fascinated horror at these happy street urchins rolling in the dust, then spent the rest of the afternoon trailing the young cockneys around the village—at a safe distance. They seemed so free and independent, with apparently no thought of their mothers and grandmothers busy with shopping, and also in long queues to buy enough food to last for a week. Vegetables, fruit, eggs, and milk they could buy at the farms, and the baker would drive his cart into the hop fields every day. Once a week a man would deliver fish, so everyone had fish and chips for supper on Wednesday.

The gypsy women were shopping, too, with enormous washing baskets hanging on their arms, but they spent very little at the butcher's because they relied on their menfolk to trap rabbits and hares. Their small children still clung to their skirts, and their fat babies were tied on their hips with colorful shawls. Rings dangled from their ears, the size and shape of curtain rings —were they brass or gold? They all wore jangling bracelets, and even the little sloe-eyed girls wore earrings and bracelets and carried babies on their hips.

We stared at them, and they stared back solemnly, but we had nothing to say to one another, for we were forbidden to speak to the gypsies.

They were a race apart, belonging nowhere, without roots. Their Romany language and way of life were as alien to us as the nomads of the Arabian Desert.

So the three separate groups of children roamed the village on Saturday afternoons, but only the cockney children of London's East End had the audacity to cheek the Vicar!

"Whatcher, guv!" They greeted him as an equal.

He coughed nervously, patted some of them on the head, while the others laughed and dodged away as he repeated, "Good day to you, dear children. Good day. Good day."

He had special prayers in church on Sunday "for our little friends from the big city"—but they preferred the Hop Pickers' Mission, with their hearty choruses and stirring exhortations to "be saved," rather than the church or chapel. The young cockneys mimicked the Vicar, as they mimicked everyone they met. "Good day to you, dear children. Good day! Good day!" We giggled gleefully in the background.

William trailed after them, hands in pockets, scowling fiercely whenever one made a playful grab at his sister.

They rolled in the road, beat one another over the head, yelled like savages, and tore the clothes off each other's backs.

"Gosh!" we exclaimed admiringly from time to time, for there seemed no limit to their outrageous antics, and no restraining hand to stop their rough play.

Then the church clock struck five, to remind us to rush home for tea so that we shouldn't miss any of the evening entertainment, which was ten times more exciting than the afternoon. By six o'clock we were back in the village, meeting our friends who had all been picking hops with their mothers at neighboring farms.

We smuggled out a bag of sweets to suck or toffees to chew and took up our positions on the churchyard wall—overlooking the Rose and Crown. The cockney children clung like limpets to the ledges and window-sills, perched on the railings, and crowded together on the steps, so the customers had to step over them with their pints of beer. They were all hugging bottles of pop and packets of potato crisps, and their shrill voices reached us on the wall. We could hear every word.

The gypsies had commandeered a separate trestle table and two benches in a corner of the forecourt.

Both men and women were smoking clay pipes.

The children hung over them, sipping beer and cider from their parents' brimming glasses, while the fat babies slept peacefully in their mothers' arms.

We devoured the colorful scene with hungry enjoyment, our jaws working through a bag of sticky assorted toffees, our tongues tasting the bitterness of almonds and the sweetness of coconut, while our eyes searched the crowded village street for familiar faces. We hailed them from the wall.

"Come on, hurry! Sit beside me—there's still room, but you're missing all the fun!"

More and more children joined us on the church-yard wall, for it was a favorite rendezvous on Saturday night in the hop-picking season.

We forgot all the work and misery of the past week in the hop fields and remembered only the fun we had escaping to the woods, collecting the water, buying apples and pears at the farm, and sheltering from the rain and sun under Mother's umbrella!

In our second-best clothes, scrubbed clean of that horrible stain, with money to spend, friends to meet, and the cockneys to watch till bedtime, we were happy again. Perched on the wall like a row of country sparrows, we joined in their songs, and with all our hearts wished we could return with them to that Big City, where children were permitted to roll in the gutter, drink unlimited quantities of pop, feed on fish and chips, and go to bed when their mothers went to bed. We could think of no better life than this!

As the shadows lengthened in the churchyard, we turned our backs on the grim gravestones, to watch the gaslight flickering across the forecourt of the inn. Lanterns were swinging from the doorposts, and the scene had the bizarre setting of a comic opera for both cockneys and gypsies became more and more animated and entertaining with every fresh glass of beer and cider.

The gypsy women and young girls were gayer now than we had ever seen them during the week and had lost their sulky furtive glances. Tossing their blue-black hair, they flirted with their men, swaying to the tune of an accordion. The sleeping babies swayed and swung in their mothers' arms, but did not wake. The accordionist played faster, and they began to sing a wild Romany song, clapping their hands and stamping their feet.

Their earrings danced and their bracelets jingled. Their faces in the gaslight held a strange and lovely ecstasy, passionate and proud. There was grace and rhythm in their movements, and the cockneys seemed crude and clumsy in comparison. The cockney mothers and grandmothers linked arms to dance down the village street, leaving the forecourt of the inn to the gypsies.

Lifting their skirts above their knees they showed

enormous thighs. "Knees up, Mother Brown!" they
shouted, and a ripple of laughter ran along the churchyard wall.

Then their children scrambled off the railings, the
windowsills, and doorsteps, leaving behind them a trail
of bottles and empty bags. They, too, linked arms and
followed their mothers and grandmothers, imitating
every gesture, the girls lifting their skirts high above
their knees, and the boys wagging their heads and shouting, "Knees up—knees up—knees up—knees up—knees
up—Mother Brown!"

The village constable leaned his bicycle against a
lamppost and smiled tolerantly. He was waiting for
closing time, when the landlord would be glad of his assistance to clear the premises before midnight.

Many of the customers who had consumed too
much liquor would be in a state of helpless hilarity and
would have to be escorted down the village street by the
burly constable and reminded to behave themselves.

It would be his duty to arrest them on a charge of
drunkenness, they were reminded, but this statement,
we were told, only served to make them even more hilar-
ious, and their shrieks of mirth often wakened us in the
early hours as they swayed unsteadily towards the farms
in the valley.

A few of the fortunate children in the village, including my friend Elsie, were allowed to stay out on
Saturday nights for this exciting climax. They told us it
was screamingly funny, for sometimes the constable lost
his helmet in the general scrimmage. Some of the customers would try to spend the rest of the night propped
against the gravestones, but the constable would not
allow such sacrilege. What would the Vicar say when he

arrived to take the seven o'clock Holy Communion on Sunday morning, supposing he found a lot of scruffy-looking customers from the Rose and Crown propping up the gravestones? He was a man of few words, the constable, but his sonorous tones conveyed authority.

Shining his torch full in their stupefied faces, he would command, "Move on! Get moving! Come on now, move on! Get moving!"

We begged to be allowed to stay up for "closing time" as we grew older, but Mother was adamant that nine o'clock was the absolute deadline.

So the weeks went by, and gradually the fields, once lovely gardens of green arcades hung with hops like grapes in a vast conservatory, were stripped bare. The mists of early autumn thickened, and the early mornings were damp and chilly.

Many of the London families demanded their wages and piled their bedding, their pots and pans, dogs, cats, canaries, and children into the farm wagons, emptied of hops, in the farmyard.

"We ain't picking no more 'ops this year, mister. We've 'ad enough," grumbled the mothers.

"We're going 'ome, mister! So long! See you next year," yelled the children as the wagons rumbled away down the lane.

"Take me back to dear old Blighty!" somebody started to sing.

Why were they always singing? They sang when they arrived, and they sang when they left, and it was their songs we remembered long after they had gone, and the village deserted: "Pack Up Your Troubles in Your Old Kit Bag, and Smile, Smile, Smile!"; "If You

Were the Only Girl in the World"; "Home Sweet Home"; and "Nelly Deane." "The Famous Duke of York" was one of our favorites, for "he had ten thousand men, and he marched them up to the top of the hill and marched them dahn again!"

Every day now the families were packing up to go back to London. It was bright lights they wanted to see again, clanging trams and shouting barrow boys. They wanted to smell the fish and chips and the smoke rising from a thousand blackened chimneys, to stand in the doorways gossiping with their neighbors. They would come again and again to the hop fields of Kent, bringing their children and their grandchildren, but after the first week or two they were always ready to go back, and some did, because they were too homesick for London.

Back to the Mile End Road and the Elephant and Castle, back to the noisy, dirty, unhealthy slum they called "home" because they belonged there, and would not exchange it for a cottage in the country. Clean, fresh country air was poison to their lungs, they told Mother with comic exaggeration! Country lanes a nightmare after dark. Who could make them understand that a rabbit was more frightened than they, or a cow mooed suddenly only when she was startled, or the screech in the barn was not somebody being murdered but merely an owl?

As the last Hop pickers' Special steamed out of the station, we stood forlornly on the deserted platform waving farewell.

Then turned away sadly, to climb the hill and to continue with the pattern of our own quiet, orderly lives —in an atmosphere of genteel poverty.

10
The Vicarage

I left the village school on my fourteenth birthday—and started work at the vicarage three days later. The Vicar's wife had lost no time in calling on Mother to beg for my services, since she had been told by the headmaster I was a nice bright girl!

Her powers of persuasion were so forceful, even Mother found herself consenting, although, as she afterwards explained to me a little self-consciously, "I have no intention of allowing you or Mary to go into domestic service. Surely you know better than that? It's just a temporary arrangement until I can find a nice little job for you."

"What sort of job?" I persisted dubiously. "Not a shop—please Mother—I don't want to be a shop girl —or an office—I don't want to be a clerk."

"What do you want, Sarah?"

"I don't know! I just don't know!" I wailed. She sighed.

"It's so difficult to place a girl, especially in a village, and you are much too young to go away from home. There is only domestic service, shop, or office work for girls. Of course there is much greater scope for boys."

"Of course," I said with bitterness.

We had been all over it so many times, and every time the answer was the same, and the argument ended in tears.

"I'm sorry, Sarah, but I haven't the means to send you to grammar school. Yes, I know you passed your exams, and the school uniform would suit you, but it's out of the question. Now, if your father was alive . . ."

"*He* wouldn't make me leave school at fourteen! He would send me to grammar school! It's not fair! I wish I was a boy! I hate being a girl! I shall run away! It's not fair! If Father was alive I should go to Baghdad and have native servants to wait on me. He wouldn't expect me to be a servant! He would understand—you don't, you never understand!"

I ran upstairs and flung myself on the bed in a storm of weeping.

I was often flinging myself on the bed these days and soaking the pillow with my bitter tears.

Standard Six was the highest peak of attainment, and I had already been sitting there for two years. I must go. We had been twice through the Colonial Empire and the history of the Romans; dwelt very briefly on decimal points and compound interest; repeated parrotwise the same two poems of William Blake and Wordsworth (but completely ignored Shakespeare). We had digested whole pages of the Old Testament and were as familiar with the Psalms and Gospels as with Robin Hood and his Merry Men. We could write legibly, providing we had a ruled page, and read aloud in singsong voices the torn ink-smudged grammars—or find the capital of China on a map of the world.

As for the birds and the bees, I knew all about them —well, almost. They were male and female, and their eggs were fertilized. I knew when they bred and why they bred but not how they bred, for that was still a dark secret.

Lambs and calves and young foals—I had seen them all, tottering and swaying on their spindly legs soon after birth. But I had not seen them born—it was too indelicate.

Babies had been born while I spent a week with a kind neighbor. When I returned home, Mary and Henry had been delivered, like two little cherubs, straight from Heaven.

"Where do babies come from, then?" I had demanded of Elsie one hot summer afternoon in the hayfield some time ago.

Elsie turned her head and looked at me kindly and protectively.

"Ma says I'm not to tell," she hedged.

"But you must, or I shall never know the answer," I insisted. "You are my best friend, aren't you?" She nodded vigorously. "Well, then?"

I waited. "Well, it's kissing that starts it," she explained mysteriously. "Don't never let a strange chap kiss you, see?"

"No, I don't see!" I snapped.

But she refused to say another word.

"Mother, what shall I do at the vicarage?"

"Oh, just make yourself useful in a general sort of way."

"You mean like a servant?"

"Well, yes, in a way." Now Mother was hedging. What was the matter with everyone lately? Why couldn't I get a straight answer—yes or no—right or wrong—true or false?

A servant was a servant, wasn't she?

"I've told the Vicar's wife you are not very strong and you are not to do any scrubbing," said Mother appeasingly.

But I was going into "service," and I had swanked to my friends it would never happen to me. Never, never!

"Good service," they called it, and it was the only work available to the humble village girl when she left school at the age of fourteen.

But I was not humble. I was proud, ambitious, and independent!

The houses of the Gentry had already absorbed several of my school friends, who lived in the cottages on the big estates, as they had absorbed their mothers and grandmothers before them. They had no choice. It was ordained from birth.

"But don't you see, Sarah, they are our Gentry, and we belong to them?"

"No, I don't see—they haven't bought you, like slaves, have they?"

"I'm going to start as a scullery maid," Ellen told me. "Then, perhaps, in a year or two I shall be a kitchen maid, and perhaps even a cook one day."

I pulled a wry face. "A scullery maid. How can you

bear it, Ellen? Washing all the pots and pans and scrubbing floors—what a horrid job!"

She smiled complacently. "I don't mind."

Alice and Fanny were starting as under-housemaids at Cowley Manor next week. We all left school the same day. They were so pleased and proud, you would think they had been invited to Buckingham Palace.

In the servants' hall, they would sit down to meals with the butler, footmen, housekeeper, housemaids, kitchen maid and parlormaid, and four gardeners. Didn't I think it was wonderful? No, I didn't. I thought a lifetime of domestic service a most appalling prospect and told them so. They laughed at me, like two children who were going on a picnic.

"You are funny, Sarah, and you do say the queerest things sometimes. It's almost like you don't belong, you know, sort of halfway between the Gentry and the likes of us."

They both hugged me and wished me luck and hoped my mother would soon find me work I really liked. Then we parted and went our separate ways.

They went gladly and willingly because they had finished with "books and learning" forever.

And I hid my despair and heartache in a cocky bravado that deceived all but Elsie—the friend of my bosom. Dear Elsie—she knew exactly where she was going and what she wanted to do with her life. She had known for years and could hardly wait to get there. Had she been permitted by the Board of Governors, Elsie would have left school when she was ten and been perfectly content with her education.

She was going to be a nursery maid to Mrs. Harold Johnson-Smythe's nanny. Mr. Harold Johnson-Smythe was a J.P., and they lived in a beautiful Elizabethan manor house three miles from the village. Elsie would live in, of course. They had four young children, and Nanny was an old tartar, judging by her appearance and her forthright manner as she marshaled her charges into the family pew on Sunday morning. But Elsie was thrilled at the prospect. She adored little children and almost always came out strung with younger brothers and sisters, nephews and nieces. Only when we went to Girl Guides could I be sure of getting Elsie on her own, for she even brought young Bert and Sylvie to Band of Hope.

"A nursery maid!" I scoffed—because I could not bear to think of Elsie living three miles away, and only seeing her for an hour on Sunday afternoon. "But it's hard work, Elsie. Nothing but washing and ironing and scrubbing nurseries and cleaning prams. And you will have to obey that awful old battle-axe of a nanny!"

"I shall love it," said Elsie convincingly, and I knew in my heart she was speaking the truth.

But when I told her about the vicarage, she was quite dismayed, and she said she thought it was a shame, because I wasn't cut out for domestic service.

It boosted my deflated ego to have Elsie think so highly of me.

I went home to Mother to ask more questions about my own dismal prospects.

"Mother, they won't expect me to wear a servant's cap and apron, will they?"

"Well, it is customary." Again she hedged.

"Didn't you tell her, then, about the uniform?"

"It wasn't mentioned." I sighed with exasperation.

"Well, I'm not wearing a cap anyway!"

"All right, no cap," Mother agreed with unusual alacrity.

"And it is only temporary?"

"Yes, only temporary."

"And I needn't do any scrubbing?"

"No, no scrubbing."

"Very well, then. I just wanted to know where I stand, that's all!"

She turned her face away—her firm mouth quivering uncontrollably. I thought she was going to cry.

"Mother, don't! It's all right. I'm sorry. Please forgive me. Oh, I'm such a pig! Such a horrid little beast! You mustn't be upset, dearest, dearest Mother! Why, it's a wonderful job! I shall love every moment, honestly! It will be the greatest fun! And the Vicar is such an old pet, isn't he?"

I kissed her stricken face and hugged her passionately.

We were seated around the kitchen table at eleven o'clock the following Monday morning. Cook had made a plate of scones and brewed a big pot of tea.

"Sit down, Sarah, over there," she said briskly.

"Where's your cap, then? Didn't the mistress give you one?" asked Jane, the housemaid.

"Mother does not wish me to wear a cap," I informed her haughtily, then added for good measure, "I'm not staying long, it's only temporary."

"Hoity-toity, miss!" said Cook, pouring tea for Graves, the butler.

"Pride comes before a fall," Annie, the parlormaid, reminded me.

"'Eaven preserve us!" muttered the gardener from behind his *Daily News*.

"Yer wanna watch yerself, Sarah Shears. Getting above yer station," said young George, the gardener's boy, who also had left school last week.

"I don't care! I haven't any station, and I don't know what you mean, anyway. I'm going to travel, like my father—and I'm going to be a famous authoress!"

They were tickled to death.

"Isn't she a scream?" "Did ever you hear such talk?" "Hoity-toity, miss!"

And I blushed uncomfortably as I nibbled my hot buttered scone.

I'll show them, I thought.

"Come along, Tweeny," said Graves. "We have work to do." I followed his ponderous figure obediently out of the kitchen.

"Why do you call me Tweeny?" I asked.

"Because you are betwixt and between."

"Betwixt and between what?"

"The housemaid and the parlormaid, of course."

How dreadful, I thought.

No status at all?

"Oh, there you are, Graves!" shrilled the Vicar's eldest daughter, bearing down on us with a large tray spilling over with daffodils and narcissi.

"What can I do for you, Miss Dorothy?" asked Graves deferentially.

She looked past him to the small figure in the long white apron and cocked her head.

"Yes, it is a teeny-weeny bit too long, Sarah. Come with me and I will find you another."

I followed her dutifully to the linen room, and she gave me another apron barely an inch or so shorter than the first.

It completely enveloped me and was so stiff with starch I could hardly bend.

Then she took out the matching cap, but I shook my head firmly and began, "Mother says—"

"Very well, very well." She seemed annoyed at my persistence, but she put it back on the shelf.

I heard her speaking to Cook about it later in the day.

"That young madam needs to be taken down a peg or two!" Cook replied.

"When you address the Vicar's daughters, you say, Miss Dorothy, Miss Agnes, Miss Millicent, and Miss Harriet," Graves pointed out. I pretended not to hear.

Millicent and Harriet were away at boarding school and expected home for the Easter holidays. They were about my own age, and very snobbish and stuck-up.

The tray of flowers was standing on the table in the pantry—golden daffodils, with the sunlight in their petals, and waxen-white narcissi, with a sweet scent.

I was still admiring the flowers when the Vicar's daughter came back to collect them.

"Mother loves flowers, we have no garden—could I —may I?"

"Oh, I suppose so. Take half a dozen of each," she said carelessly and went away again to get the vases.

"Thank you! Thank you very much!" I called after her. But she called back sarcastically, "Then, if you have time, you might go upstairs and help Jane with the bedrooms, mightn't you?"

"I will," I promised. But first I had to select the flowers for Mother and put them safely on the window-sill in a jam jar.

Then, feeling quite lighthearted, I raced upstairs,

tripping over my long apron and giggling to myself. The flowers were beautiful, Mother would love them.

It was a sort of peace offering.

I could see the golden sunlight in the daffodils and smell the sweet scent of the narcissi—yet another to add to my collection of smells. As the warm smell of geraniums in a conservatory would always remind me of Grandmother—a French perfume of the swanky Auntie —the clean smell of wind-blown washing of Mother— Pear's soap of the little ones—sour mortar in the plaster of the landlord—cider apples in the barn of Sunday School treats—pine needles and wet moss of Good Friday picnics—Icilma of the Auntie who smells nice—so I would remember the sweet scent of narcissi and the vicarage.

Such a conglomeration of smells! Some sour, some sweet, but all nostalgic.

"Thought you was never coming," said Jane in the Vicar's dressing room. "'Ere, you start on the polishing, and I'll clean them windows. You can polish, I suppose?"

She handed me some clean rags and a large tin of Ronuk.

"Of course I can polish. I know how to do most things. Mother taught me, and I went to the Housecraft Center last year. I can make pastry and shepherd's pie and fairy cakes. It was fun, we went every Wednesday for a whole year. Mother says—"

"'Ave you started on that polishing?" mumbled Jane. She gave me a withering look, but I didn't wither. I had to talk to someone.

"Do you like it here, Jane?" I asked her.

She shrugged her thin shoulders, "S'all right."

I pressed on, regardless of her uncompromising back. "Do you get Sunday afternoon and evening free?"

"Yes, from two o'clock."

"So will my friend Elsie. She's going to be a nursery maid at the Old Manor. She's my best friend, you know. We've been friends for ages and ages, and now I can only see her on Sunday afternoons. She will have to give up the Girl Guides and Band of Hope and everything. Isn't it a shame? She's my best friend, too."

I sighed. Jane shook the wet chamois leather vigorously. Her lack of interest in my affairs was rather chilling.

"What do we do next?" I asked her.

"The mistress' bedroom, and watch out it's done proper, for she's mighty particular."

"I like the Vicar, he's an old pet—but I don't like her," I confided.

"No more do I." She gave me a sly dig in the ribs, and we both giggled. "Got to start on the spring cleaning soon," she told me. "It fair breaks yer back, lifting all they 'eavy carpets and beating 'em in the yard." She sighed with resigned gloom as she stripped off her mistress' bed.

"Does every room in the house have to be spring-cleaned, then?"

"From top to bottom, even the attics."

"Gosh! it must take simply ages?"

"Six weeks or thereabouts."

Six weeks of spring cleaning? That plus six weeks of hop-picking wouldn't leave me an awful lot of time for other things—more interesting, more important things.

"Mother gets her spring cleaning done in six days —but of course it's a much smaller house," I admitted in all fairness.

"Not 'arf!" said Jane. "There's seven bedrooms in

this 'ouse, not counting the spare room, and the servants', then there's the dining room, drawing room, the master's study, the mistress' sitting room, the butler's pantry—Cook does the kitchen and scullery. Then there's the 'all and all them stairs, back and front, then right at the top of the 'ouse there's the schoolroom, the old nursery, the box room and attics, and the servants' bedrooms. You ain't seen nothing yet, my girl, but you come just about right to 'elp out, that I will say."

It certainly seemed a gigantic task, even with Annie to help, but I promised to do my best.

"Miss Dorothy and Miss Agnes is supposed to 'elp, but they don't do no more than get in the way. Miss Dorothy don't take kindly to 'ousework—don't even make 'er own bed. She's what you would call an outdoors person, likes mucking about with the chickens and the ducks and taking the dogs for a walk and such like."

"What does Miss Agnes do, then?"

With all the housework, cooking, and gardening accounted for, I wondered how she managed to pass the time.

"She's an angel, is Miss Agnes," said Jane fervently, as though nothing more was expected of her.

"A ministering angel, that's what she is. Drives 'erself, in that governess cart in the stable yard, winter and summer, in all kinds of weather." Jane paused, musing on the angelic Miss Agnes.

"But what does she do?" I persisted.

"Takes soup to the poor and needy and flowers to the sick, and always a kind word and a smile for everyone."

"You like her very much, don't you, Jane?"

"Worship the ground she walks on," said Jane reverently.

"And the others—Millicent and Harriet?"

"Ah, that's quite another kettle of fish. Turns the 'ouse upside down, they do, in the 'olidays, and such a lot of waiting on as you never did see in all your born days—proper little madams! The Vicar spoils them, that's the trouble. Fair dotes on them two youngest girls. Glory be! There's the gong for lunch, and the mistress' bedroom only 'alf finished. I shall get ticked off proper!" Jane giggled as she straightened her crooked cap. "Be a good girl and take them mats downstairs, will you, Sarah? Give 'em a good shake in the stable yard, and put a bit of polish on the floorboards. We 'ave our dinner when the others is finished. I'll give you a call when it's ready." She ran downstairs, in a flurry of skirts, her apron crackling around her calves.

I smiled at my reflection in the mirror—a diminutive figure in pigtails enveloped in a white starched apron. Then I sat down on the wide cushioned window seat, hugging my knees.

It wasn't too bad, after all, and I rather liked Jane. Perhaps we could have a bit of fun together over the spring cleaning, though the other maid, Annie, seemed rather prim and proper, and we should have to watch out for the pompous Mr. Graves. A crippling pain shot through my stomach, and I moaned as I rocked from side to side, pressing my hands to the bulge under my apron.

"Anyone would think that girl was pregnant," I had heard a spiteful woman tell her neighbor a short time ago. And pregnant meant "bearing a child." I found the word in the dictionary Uncle John have given me.

But I hadn't kissed any strange men, and neither had I started the mysterious "periods" I heard the girls discussing in the Housecraft Center.

Apparently the two went together to produce the pregnancy—the kissing and the blood. Birth was a mystery as frightening and inevitable as death—if nobody would explain it to me.

So it couldn't possibly be a baby. But it was the worst pain ever. Perhaps, I thought, if I sit absolutely still, it will get better soon?

I mustn't tell Mother, though, or she will think I am doing it deliberately.

After a few moments the agonizing pain subsided into a nagging ache, rather like toothache, but I felt sick and dizzy, and I was frightened the pain would return if I moved.

Cautiously I slid off the window seat, picked up the mats, and crept down the back stairs.

My feeble shaking dislodged no dust, but I promised myself to do better on the morrow.

Spreading a thick layer of polish on the most conspicuous floorboards, I retired from the room, satisfied that the permeating smell would quickly reach the nose of the mistress of the house!

Cook had made a steak and kidney pie for our dinner, and the pastry was the kind that melts in the mouth. The top of the pie had all the professional touches demanded by our late Housecraft mistress, but Mother thought it was a waste of time.

The edges were scalloped like lace, and a circle of pastry leaves decorated the center. The succulent juices gave out such a savory smell as the pie was opened. Graves remarked ponderously, "The master remarked on the excellence of the kidneys in the pie today, Mrs. Connolly."

"Thank you, Mr. Graves, I'm sure."

The cook blushed with pleasure. They were ingratiatingly polite to each other, I noticed, and Graves, it seemed, was always served first.

I came last but one; George, the gardener's boy, was last of all.

Annie, the parlormaid, tossed a glance in my direction as I sat down.

"You look a bit washed out. Feeling all right?"

"I'm all right, thank you." We exchanged a fleeting smile.

"May I have a small helping, please?" I ventured when my turn came.

Cook snorted, and piled the plate with pie, cabbage, and potatoes. "You could do with a bit of fattening up, strikes me, my girl!" and she slapped it down on the table.

Tears pricked my eyes, and the food choked me.

It had been agreed that I should work from eight o'clock till six o'clock, six days weekly, and have Sundays free to go to chapel, meet my friends, and take the usual walk with Mother, Mary, and Henry. My wages had also been agreed upon, without consulting me—ten shillings a week, plus food.

I already anticipated that wonderful moment when I handed to Mother my first wages—and she handed me back half a crown!

She had suggested that she start saving a regular half a crown a week for me, out of my wages; not for the proverbial rainy day but for the splendid day when

I should be launched into a career. Both the career and the launching, as vague and unspecified as my own future plans, served to keep me both dutiful and optimistic. Like Mr. Micawber, Mother was convinced that "something would turn up" during the next decade.

I could not bear to see her resolute faith and courage even momentarily shattered by my waywardness, so to curb my rebellious spirit, I poured out my anger, my grief, and frustration on paper—then tore it into a thousand pieces and tossed it out of the window! The insatiable curiosity that had so irritated my brother William when I was very young became a furtive groping after knowledge of a different kind.

Unanswered questions hammered in my subconscious mind, even when I slept.

Where do babies come from?

How does a girl become pregnant?

Why did my breasts not develop?

Why hadn't I started my "periods," when Connie Smith, who was only eleven, already boasted of this adult achievement?

What was wrong with me?

Why did nobody explain the mystery of sex? If sex was a dirty word, why was it dirty? If nakedness was wicked, why did God allow Adam and Eve to remain naked in the Garden of Eden?

"They covered their nakedness and were ashamed," I read. Yes, but that was after Eve had stolen the apple.

Nothing made sense, not even the Bible.

Uncle John was the most reliable source of information, and his theories on science, religion, and politics most interesting. Words could be defined by searching the dictionary.

But I was still searching for knowledge on the most

elementary of subjects—the birth of a child.

We had no public library, so books about matters of an intimate nature were unobtainable. The book-shelves at home contained only Mother's Sunday School prizes, her children's Sunday School prizes, the Bible, *Pilgrim's Progress*, *Uncle Tom's Cabin*, *The Swiss Family Robinson*, *The Snow Goose*, Grimm's and Andersen's *Fairy Tales*, *Little Women*, *Studies in Wild Birds*, *Studies in Wild Flowers*, and the *Children's Encyclopedia*.

Not any one of these explained the wonder, the mystery, and the altogether frightening complexity of human birth.

Uncle John would know, of course. He knew everything.

But I was too shy to ask, and we never talked of birth or of death.

These two subjects were avoided like the plague, and if touched upon, were skillfully directed into other channels both by Mother and Uncle John.

That Mother was shy on these subjects was understandable, but that Uncle John should be shy was curiously baffling—when you considered that he bred hundreds and hundreds of chicks every year in incubators on the farm. And he killed the old hens with his bare hands! So gentle a man, yet so ruthless, to kill a dear little hen with his bare hands. He would not allow us to witness the slaughter, but we knew it happened frequently, for we found the plucked feathers lying on the earthen floor of the hut.

Was he shy then only of *human* birth, as Mother was shy? Why then, were other girls so well informed, and behaved so mysteriously? I felt my ignorance shameful.

It could only mean that other mothers had other

views and principles, and were not shy or embarrassed by this important function of human birth. I still believed Mother was the most wonderful mother in the world, but now I discovered she was not completely perfect. To ignore this vital, elementary truth, that her daughters were growing into adolescence without any indication of its potential dangers, was not only unwise but incomprehensible. For if neither Mother nor Uncle John, friends, nor books could explain the mysterious functioning of our young bodies—had we then to experiment to discover the truth?

I was sent to start on the old nursery on the top floor of the vicarage as soon as we had finished a hurried breakfast of kippers the following Monday morning. Spring-cleaning fever had broken out in a rash all over the house, and I was supposed to be smitten with the malady as soon as I set foot in the servants' entrance— but I remained immune for the whole of six weeks.

With lighthearted abandon, I ran gaily up the back stairs humming a little tune I had picked up from George, the gardener's boy.

He was always whistling it.

It was called "The Lark in the Sky."

"Have you heard the legend about the lark?" I asked him one day, in the stable yard, where we idled away a few stolen moments reminiscing on our school days.

George shook his head. He was not very intelligent and had got no further than Standard Five at school, but he had what we called "green fingers," and everything he planted in his allotment grew to tremendous proportions, even the radishes.

"Well," I began dramatically, leaning on the yard

broom, "on the morning of the Resurrection . . ."
George blinked his watery eyes and shuffled his feet, for
he was not religious and had always found the Bible
quite beyond his understanding. But I persisted nevertheless.

"On the morning of the Resurrection, which was
Easter Sunday, before the Angel Gabriel appeared from
Heaven to roll away the stone, all the world was hushed
and still. It was the hour before dawn, in the garden of
Joseph of Arimathaea.

"Now, Joseph of Arimathaea had given his own
tomb for the body of Jesus, which was laid in the tomb
on Good Friday, after the Crucifixion.

"You remember that part, don't you, George?"

"I dunno. I reckon so," said George doubtfully, so I
proceeded.

"Well, just on the stroke of dawn, the Angel Gabriel appeared, to roll away the stone, and Jesus walked
out of the tomb dressed in a long white robe. All the
flowers in the garden instantly opened their petals, and
the sweet scent of the lilies was so—so intoxicating, Jesus
smiled.

"Then all the birds woke up and began to sing, for
they knew that something wonderful had happened. But
the lark was the first to fly out of her nest in the middle
of this beautiful garden, and suddenly she discovered
she could fly straight up in the sky, like . . . like an
arrow.

"Up and up she flew, singing a new song she had
never sung before.

" 'Christ is risen! Christ is risen!'—that's what the
lark was singing for all the world to hear. And still, to
this day, the lark soars upwards as swift as an arrow,
and if you listen carefully at dawn on Easter Sunday,

you will hear 'Christ is risen! Christ is risen!' from away up in the sky."

I waited for George's comment, but he was even more inarticulate than usual.

"Sounds a bit queer to me," he said. "Reckon it's time we got back to work."

The old nursery, where once the Vicar's four daughters played with their dolls under the watchful eye of their nurse, was left untouched but for annual spring clean.

The dolls still slept in cots and cradles or arranged themselves on the chairs.

A beloved teddy bear with a flattened nose sat disconsolately on the wide cushioned window seat. I dropped the brooms and brushes with a clatter to the floor and gathered him up in my arms.

We sat down together to admire the view: green fields sprinkled with little white daisies, and brown fields lined with long straight furrows, cherry orchards and spinneys, country lanes winding between tall hedges, the spire of a church, cottages and farms, sheep and cattle grazing on green pastureland—and a solitary man with a plow and a team of horses, surrounded by a flock of circling seagulls. In the kitchen garden, I caught a glimpse of young George planting out another row of cabbages, and the Vicar strolling back and forth across the lawn, his thin shoulders hunched, his hands clasped under the dark cloak that was flapping around his angular figure.

Poor man! He was probably driven outdoors to escape from a houseful of women with spring-cleaning fever.

His buxom wife was rushing around like a general

on the eve of battle, giving orders, then countermanding them. She was a great reformer and a pioneer of women's rights, but whether her servants were included in her campaigns was doubtful. Certainly they were expected to be both obedient and humble.

But I had escaped her eagle eye for the moment and had time to sit on the window seat in the nursery, watching the white birds swooping and crying, time to reflect on my status as between maid, time to ride the rocking horse and cuddle the teddy bear!

The Vicar, who could never remember names, called me simply "child" and patted me on the head when we passed on the stairs.

But the Vicar's wife, who had a penetrating voice that could not be ignored, was now calling imperatively, "Sarah! Sarah!"

I stuck my head around the door and answered, like Samuel, "I am here. Did you call?"

"Ah, there you are!" she gasped, breathless with her long climb up the back stairs.

"Who told you to start on the nursery?"

"Jane."

"Jane? But she knows very well I gave orders to start on the Vicar's study. Really! I do wish Jane would listen. Such a waste of time; she knows we always start on the study. Well, come along down, Sarah. Bring all your things, that's right. Close the door behind you."

We started down the stairs. She was still talking and explaining about the study.

George would bring me the stepladder, and I could start dusting the books. Every one must be taken out, carefully dusted, and put back.

The study was lined with bookshelves from floor to ceiling, so there must be hundreds of books, but I liked the feel of books, and anyway it was better than beating mats in the stable yard or cleaning those horrid brass stair rods. The books were heavy, and some were yellow with age, dating back more than a hundred years.

Some were printed on stiff parchment, some in Latin and Greek—and, of course, theology and academic subjects quite beyond my understanding—but I found much to interest me in the Vicar's study.

"Do be careful, child!" he called out testily when he came upon me sitting on top of the stepladder examining the doctrines of Saint Paul the Apostle! I could see he was tired of taking walks and longing to get back to his study to browse among his books and prepare his sermon. Such a scholarly man, to be a village parson. His sermons were wasted on both the Gentry and the villagers.

After lunch, Graves was waiting for me in the butler's pantry. He wore a green baize apron and looked very businesslike. The silver had been collected from all over the house, and it was our job to clean it.

"That's right, Tweeny, sit you down."

I sat down and awaited instructions.

He, too, had a collection of clean rags and an assortment of small brushes. He was mixing a pink powder with water in a saucer, and I could see it was going to be a long and laborious afternoon. He was very particular and very proud of the silver. It had to shine like a mirror before he was satisfied.

I didn't care much for Graves, or for cleaning the silver, but Cook had made some delicious chocolate éclairs for tea, and she gave me two because Graves told her I was a good girl.

Several times during the spring cleaning, I had a

sudden agonizing pain, but I managed to pretend it was indigestion, and Cook insisted that I take a good dose of bicarbonate of soda and keep off cabbage for a bit!

The pains really frightened me now, and I began to dread each fresh attack and to wonder again if I was going to die? God was punishing me now, I thought, for being so beastly to Mother.

And I was only pretending to like my work at the vicarage.

In my heart, I was still rebellious, still determined to spread my wings and follow in Father's footsteps, still determined to write a world-shattering novel or a poem of such significance it would be included in the twentieth-century anthology!

If I should die, should I leave an epitaph? I searched my mind for something suitable as I washed the pictures in the butler's pantry.

"Many daughters have done virtuously, but thou excellest them all."

Did that seem a little pompous? A trifle conceited perhaps?

"A good name is rather to be chosen than great riches, and loving favor rather than silk and gold." I decided on the latter.

Then, one hot afternoon, we were on the last lap of the spring cleaning, and, still as lighthearted as ever over this orgy of cleaning, I sat on the stepladder in the hall, flicking a feather duster over the paneling.

Pain gripped me so suddenly and violently in the stomach, I screamed out in agony and sat there, hunched on the steps, crying helplessly, till Cook and Graves, Jane and Annie ran panting into the hall from all directions, expecting to find me prostrate on the floor.

"Now, now, Tweeny, take it easy," said Graves kindly, lifting me down, while the three women stood around asking me where it hurt.

"Here, in my stomach," I whimpered, clutching it with both hands. "Mother—I want my mother."

"What shall we do with 'er, then?" I heard Jane asking anxiously.

"If only the mistress was here!" lamented Cook, wringing her hands.

"Best get a doctor," Graves decided. "Annie, send George for the doctor, and you, Jane, don't stand there gawping. Fetch her mother!"

He sent them flying in all directions. Then I found myself on a sofa, with Cook fussing over me with a blanket and a hot-water bottle.

I was shivering with cold one moment and burning hot the next.

Dimly I recall the doctor's gruff voice dismissing them all from the room, and his hands gently probing my stomach. Then he pulled up a chair and sat down, patting my hand, to ask me some questions.

Mother's stricken face swam into focus, then dissolved again into the white mist all about me.

"Hospital—operation—emergency."

These words had a terrifying urgency. I began to cry again, "Mother . . . Mother . . . Mother," and she soothed me. "Don't let me die—I don't want to die."

"You are not going to die."

She cradled me in her arms, and I could smell the tang of oranges and lemons on her hands. She had been busy making marmalade when Jane pounded on the kitchen door.

"Poor child," said the Vicar as they carried me away some time later, "I fear her days are numbered!"

11
First Love

I opened my eyes to a heavenly vision. Fat little cherubs desported themselves with happy abandon in a sky of forget-me-not blue. Some were playing flutes, some harps, some dancing with garlands of flowers, some trailing long draperies around marble pillars. Then I saw they were not alone in their enjoyment, for I discovered a sylvan glen, in a midsummer setting of shady trees, and a lake with the dazzling brilliance of diamonds.

Groups of voluptuous women reclined under the trees in indolent poses, their arms curled gracefully over their heads. Their naked bodies had the clean and clear perfection of alabaster statues.

A man and a woman lay together on a bank near the water's edge. The woman was smiling enigmatically as she dangled a ripe apple over the lips of the man.

Overhead, the branches drooped heavily with bright red apples polished by the sun.

This was not Heaven. Surely this was the Garden of Eden?

My parched mouth craved for an apple, but nobody took any notice of me, and when I tried to reach up my arm to the tree, I felt my two hands held fast, and I was a prisoner in a tight cocoon, held fast by my two hands.

The cherubs swam in a mist of tears as they teased and beckoned with their gay little flutes and flying streamers. Now I could hear them calling, "Sarah! Sarah!" Someone was patting my cheek and stroking my hair. I felt my hands clasped in other hands, warm and strong and comforting. My eyes traveled slowly down from the heavenly vision and focused on my two hands.

They were lying apart on a bright scarlet blanket, closely entwined in the fingers of two other hands I dimly recognized.

"Sarah . . . Sarah, it's Mother."

"Mother?"

She lifted my hand to touch her face, and it was real.

Now that I had seen her and touched her, I was satisfied. My eyelids drooped. The cherubs beckoned.

"Sarah! Sarah!" Mother's voice had a frightened urgency. Her deep dark eyes held mine appealingly against the sweetness of eternal sleep.

I moved my lips, but no sound came. I watched her tears trembling on her lashes, then each one, like a solitary pearl, roll slowly down her cheek.

I turned my head, to find my other hand still

warmly clasped in Uncle John's. "Hello," he said. Nothing more—just "Hello."

Then he beckoned with his finger to someone I could not see.

At the foot of the bed appeared three figures in white, but I knew now they were not angels.

The young doctor in the center reminded me of William, the two nurses were very pretty.

They all seemed extraordinarily pleased with me.

"Isn't she marvelous!" "My word, you gave us a fright yesterday, young lady!"

"Water," I gasped.

The young doctor grinned—and it was William's grin.

"Just a sip, Nurse, no more," he said.

Then they vanished behind the huge mound under which my tortured body lay encased in a tight cocoon.

Six weeks have passed, and I am impatient to go home. So many things have happened since that agonizing moment on the stepladder, I feel like another person —a ghost of my former self.

Weakness overcomes me, and I weep for no other reason than my young unblemished body is horribly scarred. The scar is an inch wide, fenced by white stripes. I have counted the stripes and there are thirty— fifteen on either side of my stomach.

I am completely obsessed by this horrifying disfigurement—not bearing to look, yet forever taking furtive glances when nobody is watching me.

When Sister had removed the fifteen stitches, she left me with a cheerful reminder that the white stripes marching down the middle of my stomach would fade within six months.

I turned my face into the pillow and wept. When Mother arrived on her weekly visit, I was still submerged, still wallowing in self-pity.

The "cottage hospital" to which I had been rushed six weeks ago was twelve miles from our village, and the visiting hours were strictly enforced, one hour on Wednesday and Sunday afternoons. Only when a patient was on the danger list were these rules relaxed. Mother had been allowed to stay at the hospital for three days and three nights after the emergency operation. Then I was considered out of danger and she returned home.

Mary and Henry had been left with our good neighbor, Mrs. Summerfield, and William was now a boarder at his school.

Mother arrived on the stroke of two o'clock every Sunday afternoon, laden with flowers, fruit, and sweets and loving little notes from Mary and Henry, my best friends, and the neighbors. I hoarded them under my pillow and read them again and again, to remind myself I still belonged to that other world beyond the walls of the hospital.

Mother took one look at my miserable face, put a comforting arm about my thin shoulders, and asked, "What's the matter?" I told her in a tearful whisper. Her eyes were tender. Her dear familiar face, worn with anxiety, had never seemed more beautiful. The hair beneath the Sunday best hat had grayed perceptibly in the past few weeks, and her eyes were ringed by dark shadows.

"Sister's right, Sarah. Those white scars will fade in a few months," she whispered back.

We kept up this whispered conversation, like two people in church, for an hour, because we were so closely surrounded by other patients and their visitors.

"But the big scar, Mother, that won't fade. It will always be there for the rest of my life, always, forever!" I whispered. "Don't you see, I'm ugly, hideously *ugly*. Nobody will love me now. I shall be an old maid!"

Mother looked into my troubled eyes and assured me that true love went deeper than that.

When the time was ripe for falling in love, I should find that a scar would probably be regarded with nothing more than compassionate interest.

But since I was still a child, why should I worry about it so soon? Everybody sent their love, even the Vicar's wife! What did I think of that?

"Oh, *Mother!*" I had to smile.

It was so funny, the clever way Mother changed the subject when she found herself in deep water!

So, to please her, I spent the rest of our precious hour together telling her amusing little anecdotes of the nurses and patients—then she would go away thinking I was no longer obsessed by the scar.

"Imagine me thinking I was in Heaven, when it was only the ceiling I was staring at!" I repeated this joke every time she came in, and it never failed to amuse her.

"Honestly, I must be balmy!"

She neither agreed nor disagreed with that statement, but offered me a boiled sweet to suck, while she unpacked a fresh supply of clean nightdresses and handkerchiefs. Then she asked when they were going to wash my hair. I said it didn't matter anyway, because I should soon be home, then she could do it herself.

She tidied the locker, put the fruit on a plate, and the flowers in my arms. It was a mixed bunch of flowers from a cottage garden, pinks, wallflowers, pansies, and mignonette.

She told me that one of the neighbors had picked the flowers while Ben was waiting at the gate with the automobile he had built with spare parts.

Ben was very proud of this new addition to his flourishing bicycle business and had offered to drive Mother to the hospital every Sunday afternoon in return for the use of our empty chicken house. It seemed a fair exchange, and Mother was grateful to accept his offer, for there were no trains on Sunday.

"I went to the hospital chapel again this morning in my wheelchair. It was so peaceful and beautiful. We sang two of my favorite hymns," I told her.

"Next Sunday, I expect I shall be able to go to our own chapel, shan't I, Mother? . . . Shan't I?" I repeated.

She was still on her knees at the locker, and she looked up with a sigh. Her eyes were troubled, her hands trembled on the red blanket.

"What's wrong? What's happened? I'm better, aren't I? Sister said I was better."

"Hush, Sarah, people are staring at us. I have some rather bad news for you. You must be brave. The doctor was waiting to see me when I came in today. He tells me they are not at all satisfied with your condition. He advised another operation. I have given my consent."

I buried my face in the pansies and mignonette.

This time, I saw no heavenly vision. I was much too busy tearing off the bedclothes and shouting for Mother. The second dose of ether had a most peculiar effect on me, and I wondered whether they had given me laughing gas by mistake. I treated the whole thing as a huge joke, laughed my head off, and sang "Onward Christian Soldiers" so many times I had to be removed to a private ward!

Mother was both surprised and embarrassed. Sister smiled behind her hand, and the young doctor with William's cheeky grin threatened to spank me if I didn't behave myself.

Uncle John, who had cycled twelve miles to the hospital and twelve miles back every Wednesday for six weeks, was delighted to have such a warm reception on the seventh visit.

I embraced him tenderly, smothered him with kisses, and assured him he was a proper old darling.

A little startled by such exuberance, he disentangled himself and his box of brown eggs to ask suspiciously, "You have had your second operation, I presume?"

"Your presumption is correct, my dear sir!" I retorted, then brushed the whole matter aside as of no consequence. "How do I look? Tell me the truth," I demanded, posing dramatically. "Do I look a mess?"

He grinned. "No, you look very pretty, as a matter of fact." I hugged him again.

"Oh, you are a darling! May I call you John? Do you mind?"

"I don't, but your Mother might!"

"Then we won't tell her. It's a secret, just between you and me. Oh, I love secrets, don't you—John? It's my favorite name, you know. You do like me, don't you?"

"I think you are a very nice and a very brave little girl."

I pulled a face. He was supposed to say, "I love you,

Sarah"—but he had missed his cue. "Oh, you are beastly to me." I pouted and stared up at the ceiling.

"Never mind, old girl. Have an aniseed ball," he suggested lightly.

Then we both shook with laughter.

Sister put her head around the door.

"Sarah Shears! If you don't stop laughing, you will split your stitches!" she reminded me with mock severity.

"Split my stitches! Ha! ha! Not split my sides, but split my stitches! Oh, isn't she a scream! Ha! ha!"

"I'm going now, Sarah. You are much too excited. Goodbye. Be a good girl. See you next Wednesday." Dropping a light kiss on my fevered brow. Uncle John departed.

Then all my elation evaporated like a pricked balloon, and I turned my face to the wall and wept.

When he returned the following week, he did not remind me of my foolishness. I was back in the main ward, and very subdued.

He sat, quietly holding my hand, talking in a low voice about the latest batch of chicks in the incubator and about the marmalade cat who had recently adopted him. He had christened him Marmaduke, and he was a splendid rat catcher.

I listened politely, and when the bell rang at three o'clock, he kissed my cheek and pushed back the chair.

"Goodbye, Uncle John. Thank you for coming." He turned at the door to wave.

Now it seemed, for the next few weeks, I was regarded as a prize exhibit, rather like a young heifer in a cattle market.

Doctors and students crowded around my bed, poked and prodded me, till I was sick with indignation.

"I want to go home!" I called after them, but they were too engrossed in their diagnosis to bother with me.

My stomach seemed to hold a peculiar fascination for all these intrepid young men, but I found it most embarrassing and huddled the bedclothes around my chin as soon as they came within twenty yards of my bed.

"Don't take any notice, dear—to them, you are just a body," said Sister complacently.

"A body, indeed!" I spluttered indignantly.

A brand new X-ray unit was installed at the hospital, and Sister offered me as a willing guinea pig.

I stood behind a glass screen to drink a pint of some revolting mixture that looked exactly like whitewash. They all said I had made history, but I felt quite sick!

My photograph appeared in the *Kent Messenger*, and friends and neighbors wrote letters of condolence—mistaking me for a corpse on a slab in the mortuary!

But the new equipment photographed well.

One morning, a week or so later, the surgeon came to look me over, with a dozen or more young students grouped about him, looking appropriately grave.

"Well, young lady, I've been getting some very good reports about you lately—a good girl, a brave girl. Splendid! Splendid!

"Now, my dear, I am going to be frank with you. The battle is not quite over, not quite. There is still one more hurdle, the final hurdle, I promise you."

What did he mean?—battles? hurdles?

"I am sending you to a London hospital, Sarah, to see a specialist. It may mean another operation. That's the spirit! Good girl! Chin up!" He pumped my hand. The students offered me weak smiles of encouragement and quietly followed the surgeon out of the ward.

• • •

For the third time, Mary and Henry were quickly dispatched to our good neighbor, Mrs. Summerfield, and Mother traveled with me to London.

She had arranged to stay with some second cousins at Hampstead, and we both found the prospect rather bleak.

Strangers to London and startled by the noise and traffic, we taxied to the main entrance of the big London hospital in complete silence, clutching each other's hands. When the time came to say goodbye, she held me close for a moment. I watched her to the door, where she turned and waved with a brave smile.

I was the youngest patient in the Raleigh Ward for women, and a short argument had taken place between a nurse and the porter before I was put to bed.

"She's only a child—she can't come in here. Take her to the children's ward, in Block Six, across the yard."

"My instructions were to bring 'er to Raleigh. Make up your mind, Nurse. Do you want 'er or don't you?"

"Oh, all right, leave her, then, and we can get it sorted out later."

I felt like an unwanted parcel of goods.

When Mother turned at the door to wave goodbye, I was frightened that within the next few moments she would be swallowed up in this big impersonal city and would disappear, leaving no trace. Her cousins had advised her to travel by taxi but, being ladies of substantial means, gave no thought to the expense. Mother had drawn her careful savings from the post office before we left. And Grandmother had sent me ten shillings.

Shivering with apprehension, I awaited my fate.

But this time Mother was "on call" for three weeks, not three days, after my third and final operation.

Poor Mother! She came and went like a quiet shadow of her former self, sitting for long hours beside my bed, holding my hand. Sometimes I was not even aware of her, and several times an urgent message was dispatched to the house at Hampstead to call her back to the hospital because I was dying.

Drooping with exhaustion, she kept her long vigil, and her dark shadowed eyes held a haunting fear that her daughter's short span of life was almost over.

Yet, as always, she was undefeated, always hopeful, always watchful for some small sign of improvement. They left her alone, the doctors and nurses, to come and go as she pleased, and admired her ceaseless devotion. She lived on cups of tea and bread and butter. The face under the Sunday best hat was gaunt and thin. Through a mist of pain, I would struggle back to see her still sitting there, and she would speak to me in a low voice and stroke my hair.

Then, satisfied, I would sink back into the half-conscious coma, with my tormented body once again encased in a tight cocoon of bandages.

At these moments of consciousness, only Mother was real—the others but shadowy figures, feeding me, washing me, changing dressings, and holding a cup with a spout to my parched lips. "Try her with beef tea, try chicken broth, try raw egg beaten up in milk, try Brand's Essence and Bovril—try anything, for God's sake!" I heard the doctor say one morning with some exasperation.

"We've got to get some nourishment into her, Sister. She's wasting away before our eyes."

"But we've tried everything, Doctor, and she does nothing but vomit!" Sister also seemed a little vexed.

It was true what they said about fading away. My

limbs were like sticks, and my ribs sticking out, and only the wad of bandages seemed to keep me from floating away altogether.

Then Mother came. I turned my head on the pillow to see her talking earnestly with the doctor and the sister.

After a few moments, she left them and hurried down the ward.

"Hello, Mother." Surprise and joy mingled on her dear familiar face.

"Thank God!" she breathed, and she kissed me with a sort of shy reverence. "It's a miracle," she said. My weak smile delighted her, and when I demanded a mirror, she found a small one in her handbag. I saw a hollow-eyed stranger, with parchment cheeks and a wispy topknot of hair. What a scarecrow! Then, my curiosity awakened at last, I asked Mother what she had been discussing with the doctor.

"Nourishment," she said. "And the doctor actually asked my advice. I felt quite flattered. But when I suggested bread and milk, both the doctor and the sister pulled a face and said they hadn't meant that sort of nourishment.

"However, I insisted that you liked it and had always asked for it when you had one of your bad stomachaches."

"Bread and milk! Oh, Mother, you are wonderful. Can I have some now?"

So bread and milk was brought, and the nurse indicated the usual little basin on top of the locker when I was ready to vomit.

Half an hour later, Sister hurried back.

"Well?" she demanded.

I proudly pointed out the empty bowl! She was delighted with the experiment and spread the glad tidings all around the ward.

Soon all the other patients were calling out to me, "Coo-ey duckie!" "How are you, luv?" "There's a clever girl!" I felt enormously pleased with myself.

The lovely summer had passed, but still the visitors brought late roses into the ward from the London florists—roses that drooped and faded within a few short hours, as I myself had drooped and faded in the ward of a big London hospital.

The sun, lost behind a maze of roofs and blank walls all day, slid down for a brief half-hour at eventide between the tall chimneys, to touch the window nearest my bed with a blaze of shimmering golden light. I watched and waited for this small miracle as one of the nurses bustled around the ward with the medicine trolley, and when she offered me a large dose of liquid paraffin and cascara, I shuddered with distaste, swallowed it quickly, and sucked a barley sugar sweet.

The sun beckoned me with warm tantalizing memories of the hayfields and Mother pouring tea from a flask—bees humming in the clover—meadows carpeted with yellow buttercups—tall foxgloves swaying on the riverbank—ripening apples in the orchards—a thrush with a spotted waistcoat singing in full-throated ecstasy on the churchyard wall at daybreak—and trees, always trees.

It was the trees I missed most of all during that long hot summer in a London hospital.

A tree, any tree, I craved to see, with an almost fanatical frenzy, as others would crave to see a mountain or a river, a London bus, or even Selfridge's store.

But who would listen to such nonsense? Who would understand if I told them I wanted a tree?

Even to myself it seemed an absurd request and sounded a little odd. I couldn't bear to be laughed at any more or teased about my peculiar fads and fancies, so I kept quiet, staring for long moments at the rooftops, the tall chimneys, and the blank walls.

There seemed no joy in anything now. Mother had returned home at the end of three anxious weeks to collect Mary and Henry from Mrs. Summerfield. William had spent most of the summer holiday bird-watching and fishing.

He wrote dutifully and formally once a week, but his letters were so brief I found no trace of his lively intelligence in the few stilted phrases. Mary also wrote regularly and lovingly, filling up the page with rows of kisses to compensate for the lack of news.

Henry, I knew, had a deep aversion to pen and paper, and the laborious task would be postponed till the last moment.

I could imagine him, disturbed from his beloved carrots and cabbages, obliged to conjure up a few bald sentences on the state of the weather and his sister's health.

He always hoped I was well as it left him at present —and this was so typically Henryish, I felt strangely comforted by this oft-repeated sentiment.

Mother traveled up to London every Sunday by train to visit me for one hour.

It was the highlight of my week, but after she had left, I crawled back into my own private little shell like a snail and drifted back to the vale of tears.

One Wednesday afternoon, I had persuaded myself

as usual that I didn't mind all the other patients having visitors, that I was neither lonely nor homesick, and I didn't care for company anyway.

Then, walking briskly down the ward, grinning boyishly, came Uncle John! My heart skipped a beat, and I knew I was blushing.

His plain freckled face seemed extraordinarily beautiful. His hair was bleached by the sun. In his tailored navy-blue suit, he looked most distinguished and, as Mother would say, a perfect gentleman. He carried an armful of bright orange marigolds and a box of eggs. Even in his best suit—I liked him best in breeches and jacket and wellington boots—he brought a breath of fresh country air into the stifling ward.

I opened my arms, and he hugged me boisterously, still with that huge delighted grin on his face.

Now I knew why I had been feeling so utterly miserable.

It was Uncle John I wanted to see more than anyone else in the world, even Mother.

It was his shoulder I wanted to cry on! John—darling John! But now I was suddenly shy of him, as of a stranger. To call him "John" seemed much too familiar, and "darling" altogether outrageous.

Oh, but he was a darling—so kind, so thoughful, so altogether nice!

"Hello, Uncle John," I managed to whisper at long last. Just that, and nothing more—"Hello, Uncle John." But he didn't seem to notice my embarrassment.

He drew up a chair and sat down, his big strong hands clasped on the red blanket.

Shyly I laid my hand on top of his.

Its waxen transparency touched on his healthy sun-

239

tanned skin was a delicacy I found quite appealing! But he folded it quickly into his warm clasp and went on talking in a low voice, carefully modulated for my benefit.

His somber gray eyes held a new shining brightness, and he seemed much younger than his thirty-five years, quite boyish in fact. I had never known him so animated and talkative. Some of his vigor and vitality flowed into me through the warm clasp of the two strong hands holding mine. All the misery, suffering, and homesickness of the past few months were forgotten. His happiness was so evident in every feature, every gesture, and his glowing health lifted me out of the vale of sickness and tears. So this was love!

This radiant transformation was all for me! I felt very humble and very privileged to be the chosen one, and deeply grateful for the honor. Breeches and muddy boots could never disguise the inherent good breeding of a cultured man.

He knew everything, I knew nothing. But soon that would be rectified, and all the burning questions answered. Ignorance would be explained. I trusted him implicitly, for he represented the very essence of integrity and balance in our family life. His high standards of morality, his impeccable behavior and sense of duty matched Mother's.

Together they had taught us, by their excellent example, the essentials of good living. I loved them both, dearly and devotedly.

Together with William, Mary, and Henry, they provided all that I now needed for complete happiness and contentment. My restless spirit no longer craved variety and excitement, and Father's adventurous way of life no longer attracted me.

I was a changed person—because of John, or because I had so many hours to contemplate the nature of things?

Strange places and strange faces had lost their fascination now that I had tasted the bitterness of separation from those I loved best. It was dear familiar faces I longed for now—like the one beside me.

He was still talking, while I listened with only half a mind. It seemed to be a long and detailed account of Auntie Harriet's visit. Mother had mentioned it, but I was too ill at the time to take much notice. It seemed that the swanky Auntie had suddenly decided to spend a short holiday with her sister in the country—to keep her company during the anxious weeks following my operation.

She had arranged to arrive on the day Mother was due back from London, but Mother was delayed by the demands of her troublesome daughter, and could not meet her. So she sent a telegram to Uncle John, asking him to meet Auntie Harriet at the station, and also to collect Mary and Henry from Mrs. Summerfield's (I wish he would talk about us).

"You are not listening, you naughty girl!" he reprimanded me playfully, and squeezed my hand so hard it hurt.

(My head ached, and I would like to lie on his shoulder.)

He carried on with the story, so I dropped my head back on the pillow with a sigh of resignation, reminding myself that Uncle John always took rather a long time to come to the point. He was not the sort of person to rush madly into a love affair, even with someone he had known for five years. His nature was careful and cautious, not impulsive like mine.

But now I had reached the age of maturity, all that would be changed, and John would see in me nothing but good common sense and a practical, balanced mind. I felt we knew each other's character and disposition so well, this should not be difficult.

It was sweet of him to have taken so much trouble with Auntie Harriet—and she not even a relation. But that was typical of John. He was polite to everyone, even the smallest child.

I watched his mobile face with blissful contentment, and reached up my free hand to stroke his hair. It was stiff as straw, and so bleached by the sun it could have been plucked from a field. "I met the train, Sarah —are you listening?—and your Auntie was the only lady passenger to step out onto the platform, so I knew it was she. Besides, you had told me so much about the aunties, and I knew the swanky Auntie wouldn't be likely to arrive looking at all dowdy or old-fashioned.

"But, believe me, Sarah, she quite took my breath away! Indeed, I wondered whether she hadn't come straight from Paris instead of Worthing! She was so elegant! Then she looked at me, and I looked at her, while the porter dragged out her luggage, and we went on shaking hands for a full five minutes!

" 'How do you do?' we said. Just that. Would you believe it? 'How do you do?' with the usual conventional politeness. But we knew, Sarah! We knew we had not met by chance.

"Call it love at first sight, if you like, but it was mutual and quite spontaneous.

"So there it is, and incredible as it may seem, we are engaged to be married at Christmas! We want you and Mary to be our bridesmaids, so you must hurry up

and get well and strong! We thought of buying the
empty cottage near the farm and settling down there.
What's the matter? Have I said anything wrong?"

Anguished tears rolled slowly down my cheeks.

My heart was broken into a thousand fragments
and lay scattered at his feet.

"I thought it was me you loved," I sobbed. "I
thought you would wait for me to grow up, and now you
are going to marry the swanky Auntie. She's got three
suitors already—she doesn't need any more! Oh, it's not
fair! How could you be so mean and beastly when you
knew I loved you?"

His bewilderment was genuine; his compassion
made my tears flow faster.

"But, Sarah, dear—you are just a little girl. I'm
terribly sorry. Please forgive me. There now, have a
good cry on Uncle John's shoulder!"

I knew it was autumn when Mother arrived the
following Sunday with a large bunch of bronze chry-
santhemums from the vicarage garden.

Kind messages had reached me from time to time
from Cook and Graves, Annie and Jane, and even young
George. It seemed a lifetime ago when I sat with them
around the kitchen table and told them of my bold ambitious plans for the future—plans I couldn't bear to
think about now without shedding a few tears of self-
pity.

It was understood I should not return to the vicarage or domestic service, but Mother would promise
nothing beyond a vague "We shall see when you are
better. Don't worry about it."

The Vicar's wife had sent in several bunches of

blue-black hothouse grapes and the neighbors had bought expensive peaches wrapped in tissue paper.

This luxury fruit made a tempting display on my locker, but I gave it away surreptitiously to the night nurses and craved only for a hard juicy apple from a Kent orchard.

"Why can't I have an apple?" I asked Sister peevishly.

"Because the doctor says you mayn't."

"A pear, then?"

"No pears, either."

"But I don't like grapes and peaches. They are so—so exotic!"

Sister shrugged impatiently.

"Exotic, my foot! You are getting to be a horrid spoiled little girl, Sarah Shears!"

"I'm sorry, Sister," I mumbled, for I was never quite sure if she meant it, and one did not take liberties with Sister.

"Well, then, you needn't look so pathetic. It's for your own good, all this careful dieting. You don't suppose we enjoy keeping you on a diet of minced chicken and egg custard, do you?"

"No, Sister." She sighed as she studied me carefully from the foot of the bed.

"I wish I knew what you do want—apart from an apple, that is?"

"I want to go home."

"Yes, that is understandable. You've been here long enough, ten weeks, in fact. But you can't go home till you can walk, and you haven't yet managed to get to the bathroom under your own steam, have you? So it's up to you, my dear child, entirely up to you. The opera-

tion was successful—it had to be, since you had one of
the finest surgeons in the country to operate. We can't
force you to eat. We can't insist that you take an interest
in other people or your immediate surroundings for a
change, but you could, you know. Just to lie there feeling sorry for yourself is not adult, it's childish. Besides,
you owe it to your mother."

Sister often gave me a lecture, but this time it went
deep.

It was up to me, she said.

My legs felt like jelly and my body so light I
seemed to be floating in space.

But I managed to reach the bathroom a few yards
down the passage.

My favorite nurse was cleaning the bath. "Why,
hello, duckie! You look like death warmed up!" she said
cheerfully.

Then she swept me into her arms and carried me
back to bed.

"You see, Doctor, Sarah is a country girl, born and
bred in a remote Kentish village," Mother was explaining patiently to the impatient young house surgeon.

"Now, if only there was a garden . . ."

"But there is a garden, of a sort," he interrupted.
"Just a couple of tennis courts, a few rose bushes, a scrap
of lawn, and, I believe, a tree."

"Ah, a tree?" said Mother brightly. "Now that, in
my opinion, would be as good as a tonic for Sarah. You
will excuse me saying so, Doctor, but sometimes a
mother knows best what her child needs. I do appreciate
all you have done for Sarah in this hospital, but might I
suggest you act on my advice now? Just let her sit in

the garden for a little while each day. Autumn is such a lovely season of the year in the country, but if there is a tree she will enjoy watching the changing of the leaves. Why, she might even write a little poem about it if she had a scrap of paper and a pencil!"

They both exchanged a smile of complete understanding, then the young doctor stepped across to my bed and playfully pinched my toes.

"Come on, lazybones! Up you get! Nurse, ask the porter to fetch a wheelchair, will you? This young lady is going out in the garden!"

"I have to leave you now, Sarah, to catch my train. You will be all right now, won't you? I thought it was high time to make a suggestion—after all, I am your mother!"

She watched while the porter wrapped me carefully in a blanket and wheeled me out of the ward.

Then she waved triumphantly from the opposite door and vanished.

It was a sycamore tree, and how it came to be growing on a small patch of sooty soil in the garden of a big London hospital, nobody seemed to know. The tinted leaves of gold and red and brown rustled in the breeze.

This rustling held for me the same kind of music as the Grieg concerto I heard played on a gramophone record a few days ago.

I was on my way to X ray, and as we passed the nurses' sitting room, I heard this beautiful music. We paused for a few moments to listen, and it was so beautiful I cried. "That was a Grieg concerto," I was told.

A few friendly little sparrows hopped and chirped around my chair, and I found a broken biscuit in the pocket of my dressing gown. The sun filtered through the branches, and I lifted my face to its warm caress.

All my senses were alert at last—and I took a crumpled letter and a pencil from the same pocket and began to write with laborious concentration on the back of the envelope:

> *It makes no sudden plunge from green to red*
> *As autumn days slip by.*
> *It likes instead to wait*
> *While others fade and die,*
> *And then to turn a shade of brown.*
> *So gradually and slowly crown*
> *Its slim indulgent self*
> *With warmer tints of glowing health,*
> *So that the sun can better shine*
> *Through colored leaves*
> *Into the chill of my small heart.*
> *God bless the trees!*

12
Jackie

"It was a tree that saved my life," I told William.

For once he did not scoff. In the year I had been away, in hospital and convalescent home, he had grown surprisingly gentle and serious. His arrogance was replaced by a manner so quiet and reserved he seemed almost a stranger. His smile was kind and tolerant, and he sat down to hear the story of this miracle, searching my face with deep brown eyes. He listened thoughtfully without interruption, twirling a lock of hair between finger and thumb. It was a gesture so familiar, and so essentially William, I was glad he hadn't changed beyond recognition.

As a great naturalist, he received the story with conviction, and agreed with Mother that trees were the very breath of life to a country-bred child. For the first time in my life, I felt he regarded me with something more than just a mild curiosity—with interest, even admiration. It did more for my morale at this stage of readjustment to family life than any other factor.

Perhaps we had both matured?

I had suffered pain, been near to dying, seen the torment and agony of sick and deceased bodies in the public ward of a big London hospital. I had learned the meaning of compassion, tolerance, and patience. It was the end of childhood, but also the beginning of a brave new chapter.

Still very weak and emotional, I wept easily, but I also found new joy in a number of things I had taken for granted. Friends and family wrapped me around in a cloak of warm affection. I was coddled and cosseted. The Vicar's wife was so appalled at my condition, she insisted on calling every day with a basin of beef tea or chicken broth—both would have made me sick, but Mother insisted it would be ungracious to refuse.

"The poor child must be nourished; she is nothing but a skeleton!" she exclaimed.

Then she asked the Vicar to call. He looked down on me from a great height, with the same kindly benevolence, and patted my head as usual.

"Dear child, my dear child," he murmured. "Shall we say a little prayer together to thank God for your amazing recovery?"

"Yes, please."

I was touched by this suggestion, and Mother knelt beside me holding my hand.

"I've been to the services in the hospital chapel in my wheelchair, and the nurses and doctors sang most beautifully. Once I was allowed to choose a hymn, and I chose my favorite, 'All Thing Bright and Beautiful,' " I told the Vicar importantly.

A Village Girl

With so much attention over such a long period, I
had grown very self-important. Everyone wanted to hear
about my experiences in a London hospital and the convalescent home, where I had spent a month after leaving
hospital. Still the center of attraction, I enjoyed my new
status and held court like a queen!

Uncle John fetched me once a week in his little
ramshackle car. The seats were usually sprinkled with
meal and maize and piled with empty egg boxes. Hanging on to his arm, I walked slowly and quietly through
the maze of huts and incubators as he explained the
mysteries of the new oil heating system and the number of chicks hatched since my last visit. In the small
galvanized hut smelling of meal and potato mash, I sat
down on an upturned bucket to fill egg boxes and talk to
my dear first love. I could see now that he hadn't
changed at all from the day he arrived at our house to
be our first lodger.

But I had changed.

In my young adolescence, I had clothed him in
romance and seen him as a lover. To see him again in
familiar surroundings, wearing his shabby corduroy
breeches and mud-caked boots, and with wisps of straw
in his hair, was in a sense a relief, for I found a very
dear elder brother restored to me, with all embarrassment over. We could laugh together over the broody
hens and strutting cocks, and kneel together on the hard-
baked earth to gather a handful of fluffy yellow chicks.
I watched him mixing the mash, then followed him
around at feeding time. He carried a bucket on each
arm, one of mash and one of grain. The grain slid
through my fingers as I scattered it in the chicken runs.
He seemed to see me with the same eyes, as the same
girl, and made no mention of my changed appearance—

I had lost most of my lovely hair, and was thin as a bean pole! He was happy with the swanky Auntie in their little cottage, and she had developed an unexpected talent for cooking.

"We live like fighting cocks!" he told me. "You wait till you taste your auntie's chocolate cake, it's out of this world!"

I told him I was still using the dictionary he had given me as a birthday present, and I had started writing a novel! He showed no surprise at this rather alarming leap from the shortest of short stories and poems. But he was like that. Never surprised, outraged, or critical— the gentlest and most understanding person I had ever known.

Our new lodger was a schoolteacher, and we had no feeling for her at all, or she for us. She was just a "lodger"—casual, condescending, and critical. There is nothing more to add, for her weak personality barely stirred a ripple in the stream of our quiet family life.

It had been arranged for me to start on my five-year apprenticeship at the village post office as soon as I was strong enough. Six months was suggested by my doctor as a necessary period of convalescence following three major operations.

It was a time of happy contentment, for I spent long hours scribbling in exercise books, without interruption or adverse comments on the shocking waste of time and paper! During this short period between childhood and the adult world of the Civil Service I was destined to enter, Mother was surprisingly indulgent about the writing. She was relieved to have my future happily settled, for her main ambition in life was still the same as ever: *security* for her children.

Then one morning she announced with typical calm that she had decided to be a foster mother. William was home for the weekend from his lodgings, Mary and Henry were still attending the village school, and we all looked at her with the same wariness as the day she had announced we were having a lodger.

A foster child would fill the gap in the family, she explained carefully, for she missed having a little one about the house, and her own children had grown up too quickly. With his new gentleness, William listened politely and observed, "Quite a good idea, actually. You always enjoyed us best when we were under your feet."

Mother smiled gratefully at her first-born, for she had expected strong opposition to her plan. Mary, of course, was delighted, for her strong maternal instinct had developed over the past year, and her idea of Heaven would be a house filled with babies.

I was dubious, and Henry indignant.

"Lines of washing and nappies all over the place and yelling kids, like the Harrisons. We don't want any more children. We are quite all right as we are," he protested stubbornly.

But Mother had made up her mind, and nothing or nobody could change it. Henry knew this, but he always tried.

"It won't be a tiny baby, so there won't be any nappies. I thought of a child about two years of age. And all little children don't yell, though you certainly did your share, Henry, but Mary was as good as gold," Mother pointed out reasonably.

"Will it be a boy or a girl?" was the only question I cared to ask, for I hadn't Mary's instinctive love of little children, or the patience to cope with them.

"We shall be notified," said Mother complacently. "I said I had no preference and would take either a boy or a girl. So many foster mothers seem to want a pretty little girl with golden curls and blue eyes. It's quite a problem to find permanent homes for the plain children, and the boys. People will have them for a time, then make excuses to hand them back to the authorities."

William was quite shocked at such callous treatment.

"Poor little devils, it's inhuman," he declared feelingly.

We still had the big old-fashioned pram and the cot we had all used in turn. We would "make do" as usual, and this didn't surprise me, for we had been making do all our lives.

Once more we all went off to the station to meet a train that would bring a new personality into our sheltered little world.

I remembered in every vivid detail the day we had waited for Father on this same platform. Today we waited for a little stranger with the same rather tense nervousness and apprehension, for he would be one of us, a member of the family, for probably the rest of our lives.

It was a serious matter, not to be lightly dismissed. We all felt and recognized its fundamental quality, of a lasting, not a temporary nature. Mother had not decided in a hurry. We knew she had given it much thought and serious consideration before she even mentioned it to her children. She was never a creature of whims and impulse, moods or temper. Her steadfastness was a rock on which to build for the future.

As the train slid to a halt, the same porter shuffled

down the platform to pull out the boxes, baggage, and mail bags from the luggage van. A woman stepped out briskly and raised a beckoning hand. We hastened towards her and peered eagerly into the carriage.

"Well, here we are at last! This is Jackie, and he's rather a pet." The woman's voice was so impersonal, she might have been handing over a parcel. Even a puppy or a kitten would have been blessed with a little more ceremony.

I felt an instinctive dislike of her and, at the same time, an overwhelming compassion for the small bundle on the seat. He was eighteen months, could neither walk nor talk, was exceptionally good, well behaved, and placid—we were told.

We stood in the doorway staring at this small paragon, while he stared back with wide solemn blue eyes. He was wrapped so tightly in a cocoon of woollies, he seemed unable to move. Beside him on the seat was a kitbag containing his entire wardrobe.

Mother's face held that same tender expression I had seen so often in childhood when I sat on a hassock at her feet while a baby suckled her breast. She was all maternal again and seemed not to hear what the woman was saying.

Getting into the carriage, she gathered the fat little bundle in her arms and stepped out carefully onto the platform. Henry climbed in and picked up the kitbag without saying a word. His stubborn mouth was trembling, and he was near to tears. Mary touched the child's cheek with a gentle hand and smiled a welcome. William stood apart, as always.

The guard waited to blow his whistle, and the woman got back into the carriage. "Can't stop! Three more children to collect in Brighton today!" she announced importantly.

As the train moved away, William raised his hat politely, then followed us down the platform.

Jackie was sitting in the pram now. It had been cleaned and polished by Henry, and the spokes glittered as they spun. He was still holding the kitbag, still absorbed in the child, but too shy to make the first contact. Eventually, conquering the shyness, he patted Jackie's hand and grinned.

"Hullo, Jackie." Henry's grin was irresistible.

The blue eyes widened, and the solemn little face dissolved in a smile. He held up his arms, and Henry, flushed with this new and strange protectiveness, gathered the heavy child awkwardly to his small chest. Staggering under the weight, he carried him to the end of the platform, then dropped him carefully back in the pram.

"Gosh! but he's awful heavy!" he panted.

"Too fat—much too fat. The wrong kind of feeding. Too much stodgy food," said Mother as she pushed the pram. "And probably bronchial. Can you hear him wheezing?" she added.

She was right, of course. Mother was always right. She nursed him through bronchitis, whooping cough, measles, and chickenpox in the next five years, and bathed his rickety legs in Steadman's Sea Salts.

I handed over my throne to Jackie, for now he was the center of attraction, and my "reign" had lasted long enough. He was a lovable little boy, but almost too angelic in the early days. Obviously he had been accustomed to sitting all day, and seemed quite shocked and surprised to find himself on the floor.

Then he began to crawl—a peculiar crablike shuffling motion. But he did not walk or talk till he was past his second birthday. His hair was the color of ripe corn, his cheeks pink, his eyes cornflower blue. He adored Henry from that very first moment, and always greeted him from school with shouts of joy and excitement, even before he spoke a single word.

I found in him a new, absorbing interest, for he was so attractive, once the flabby baby fat had gone, I was compelled to adorn him in pretty clothes. Once again the old sewing machine rattled. Little buster suits, short knickers and blouses, even a coat, took all my spare time, when I was not pushing him out in the pram.

My "novel" was left unfinished at Chapter Six, and all my emotions involved in this one small boy. Someone to love. It was enough for the moment.

But soon I should feel the old urge to spread my wings. I should be torn apart with the old conflicting forces. Mother was still the central figure in my little world, and her strong personality still dominated our home. But I knew all the time, as she herself knew, that I was essentially my father's daughter, and a rebel at heart.

The chapter of my youth had already closed. Inevitably there would be a new chapter one day. It would be called, appropriately, "Gather No Moss."

THE END